Life in Eastern Kentucky

A PICTORIAL HISTORY: 1940–1970

PRESENTED BY THE LEXINGTON HERALD-LEADER

Acknowledgments

Many thanks to the citizens of Eastern and Central Kentucky, whose sharing of their family photographs made this book possible.

The text was written by *Herald-Leader* staff writer Andy Mead.

Other photographs in this book were graciously provided by these organizations:

Bobby Davis Museum and Park in Hazard

The Appalachian Collection of the McGaw Library and Learning Center at Alice Lloyd College

Bryan W. Whitfield Jr. Public Library in Harlan

Pikeville Public Library

Rowan County Public Library

Godbey Appalachian Archives at Southeast Kentucky Community and Technical College

Transylvania University Library Archives

Special Collections at the Hutchins Library in Berea

Camden-Carroll Library Special Collections at Morehead State University

TABLE OF CONTENTS

FOREWORD

The 1940s, '50s and '60s were a time of great change in Eastern Kentucky. The terrain that had kept earlier generations cut off from the rest of the country gradually lost its isolating power as horse and foot trails gave way to blacktop. Soldiers who came home from Europe or the Pacific with broader experiences after the war took their place among the region's leaders. Televisions brought a flickering vision of the world into living rooms.

But there continued to be periods of boom and bust, and another war — on poverty — was declared. For a time, the nation's attention was focused on the have-nots in the hills, but that interest faded long before the underlying problems were solved.

What did not fade was the stubborn independence and the strong sense of family and place held by the people of Eastern Kentucky. Toward the end of the period covered in the following pages, there was a reverse migration as people who had left for jobs outside the region retired and moved back, not satisfied to spend the end of their lives in places where one could not look out a window and see lush green mountains.

As you look through the hundreds of people whose photographs are shown in this book, you are likely to see some familiar family names and maybe some relations. And, if you are of a certain age, you might find a younger version of yourself.

PUBLIC SERVICE

When Pearl Harbor was bombed, pushing America into World War II, Kentuckians signed up for the fight at a greater per capita rate than most Americans. The rate was exceptionally high in Eastern Kentucky, where many patriotic men rushed into uniform.

For many, the trip to their military base, then overseas, was their first time out of the mountains, or past the borders of their own county. Tragically, too many never made it back.

Those who stayed behind did their part. There were drives to gather scrap metal, old tires and even paper to help the war effort, and a region that had little found it had much to give. Being on the home front also meant living on rationing cards, and women stepping up to do the kind of work that had been reserved for men.

Through the early part of the years covered in this book, parts of Eastern Kentucky still were so remote that a Depression-era program was needed to get books delivered by librarians on horseback. The unique program scored a visit from an admiring First Lady Eleanor Roosevelt.

Scrap drive in Hazard during World War II. *Courtesy of Bobby Davis Museum and Park*

Hospital in Wheelwright, circa 1940. *Courtesy of Nancy Bailey Griffin*

Public Health clinic in Clark County, circa 1940. *Courtesy of Special Collections & Archives, Camden-Carroll Library, Morehead State University*

Packhorse librarians were part of the Work Projects Administration in Appalachia from 1935 to 1943. *Courtesy of Special Collections & Archives, Camden-Carroll Library, Morehead State University*

Eleanor Roosevelt visiting the display on the WPA packhorse librarian project, circa 1940. *Courtesy of Special Collections & Archives, Camden-Carroll Library, Morehead State University*

Edison J. Disney, circa 1942, from Barbourville. He was killed in Italy in October 1944. He left a wife, Jeree, and six-year-old daughter, Pat. He was from the 351st Regiment, a member of the 88th Division that was called the Blue Devils. They were named that by the German Army because of the blue cloverleaf insignia on their shoulder and the fact that they fought like devils. *Courtesy of Pat and Don Dampier*

Rescue squad from Benham at the community's annual Safety Day, circa 1940. James E. Jaco is second from the left; Clifford Smiddie is second from the right. Others are unidentified. *Courtesy of anonymous*

Serving in the military during World War II are three brothers and a cousin, left to right: Ray Creech, Harold Johnson, Earl Creech and Claude Creech.
Courtesy of Lucien H. Rice

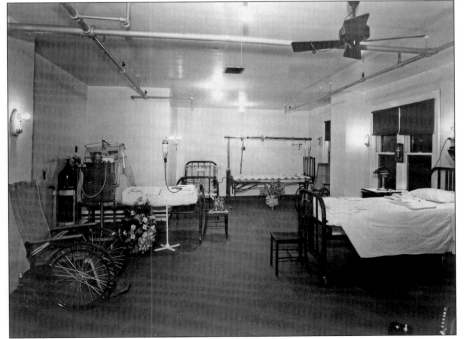

National Hospital Day exhibit at Pikeville Methodist Hospital, May 1941. *Courtesy of Pikeville Medical Center*

Raymond Richardson, left, with his friend, Cecil G. Osborne, 1943. Cecil served overseas in the Army and was probably home on leave. The young men were from Estill County. *Courtesy of Wilma Osborne Hamilton*

Quentin Fields, Lost Creek, Breathitt County, before embarking for service in the U.S. Army Air Corps. He served in the Pacific and Asiatic Theaters from 1942 to 1945. *Courtesy of Carol Fields Shepherd*

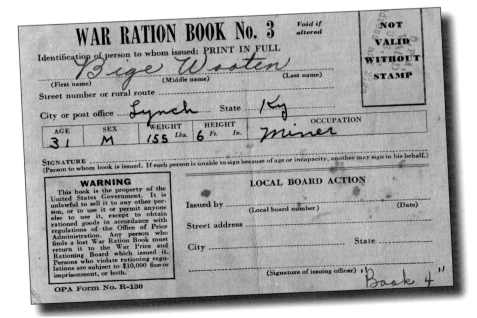

WAR RATION BOOK No. 3 Void if altered

NOT VALID WITHOUT STAMP

Identification of person to whom issued: PRINT IN FULL

Bige Wooten

(First name)   (Middle name)   (Last name)

Street number or rural route

City or post office *Lynch* State *Ky*

AGE	SEX	WEIGHT	HEIGHT	OCCUPATION
31	M	155 Lbs.	6 Ft. In.	*miner*

SIGNATURE
(Person to whom book is issued. If such person is unable to sign because of age or incapacity, another may sign in his behalf.)

WARNING
This book is the property of the United States Government. It is unlawful to sell it to any other person, or to use it or permit anyone else to use it, except to obtain rationed goods in accordance with regulations of the Office of Price Administration. Any person who finds a lost War Ration Book must return it to the War Price and Rationing Board which issued it. Persons who violate rationing regulations are subject to $10,000 fine or imprisonment, or both.

OPA Form No. R-130

LOCAL BOARD ACTION

Issued by
(Local board number)   (Date)

Street address

City   State

(Signature of issuing officer) *Book 4*

World War II ration book for Bige Wooten, Lynch. *Courtesy of Beuna Wooten*

Lt. Commander U.S.N. Edgille Hall, left, and Edward Leslie, circa 1942. Edgille was born in Weeksbury and grew up in Flemingsburg. Edgille's plane was shot down in the Phillipines in 1946. His body was never found. Ed survived the war and became a dentist in Prestonsburg. *Courtesy of Barry Dean Martin*

Joseph V. Hamilton home on leave from the Air Force with his brother, Thomas E., 1943. They are at their home in Vanceburg. *Courtesy of Mary Hamilton Adams*

Beuna, left, and Arzona Wooten with a picture of their brother, Grover C. Wooten, who was serving in the Marines in World War II. The star was put in the window of homes where there was a man serving overseas. The family was living in Cumberland. *Courtesy of Beuna Wooten*

Children helping with the scrap drive in Hazard during World War II. *Courtesy of Bobby Davis Museum and Park*

Willard "Junior" Moore Chapman Jr. with his wife, Ruby, and son Gary at his parents' home in Flatwoods, 1943. He was home on leave from training as a radio operator in the U.S. Army Air Corp. He was on the crew of the B-29 "Black Jack Too" when it was shot down over Japan on June 5, 1945. Most of the crew bailed out and then were captured a few days later. They were prisoners of war until their execution later that month. *Courtesy of Randy Smith*

Adrian Hall sent this postcard from Germany, dated May 29, 1945, to Dewey and Magnolia Martin. "Keep this card as a souvenir. This leaves me well and wishing I was home. How I miss the states and the people I know. Regards to Aunt Hebads. As ever, Adrian." Adrian survived the war and became a prominent educator and minister and raised a family in Floyd County. *Courtesy of Barry Dean Martin*

Tire drive during World War II in Hazard, circa 1944. *Courtesy of Bobby Davis Museum and Park*

Scrap drive in Hazard during World War II. *Courtesy of Bobby Davis Museum and Park*

Scrap drive in Hazard during World War II. *Courtesy of Bobby Davis Museum and Park*

Scrap drive in Hazard during World War II. *Courtesy of Bobby Davis Museum and Park*

Navy V-12 program students at Berea College, circa 1944. The young men were housed in Blueridge and Cumberland halls on campus. *Courtesy of Appalachian Photoarchives, Southern Appalachian Archives, Berea College*

Joseph V. Hamilton serving in the Air Force, 1943. He was called into service six weeks before graduating from high school. Because he was such a good student, the school issued his diploma of graduation. In his absence, Joseph's younger brother, Paul, put on an Air Force uniform and walked across the stage to accept the diploma on behalf of his brother. *Courtesy of Mary Hamilton Adams*

Willard Maggard in his Army uniform, circa 1942. He lived on Big Cowan, Whitesburg. *Courtesy of Judy Burroughs*

Dr. Pierce Martin in his treatment room at Kentucky Straight Creek Coal Co., Belva Mine, Bell County, Fourmile, Sept. 4, 1946. The mine was abandoned after an explosion in December 1945. *Courtesy of Photographic Archives, Appalachian Learning Laboratory, Alice Lloyd College*

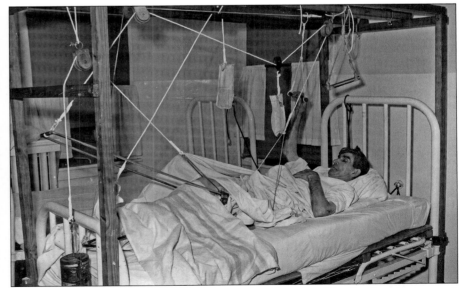

Hazard Post Office employees, circa 1946: Marion Bailey, Barney Baker, Frank Baker, Charlie Nicholson and postmaster Anna Moore. *Courtesy of Bobby Davis Museum and Park*

Hugh Pierce, miner, in the hospital in Harlan County with a broken leg caused by a slate fall in the Black Mountain Coal Co. 30-31 Mine at Kenvir, Sept. 6, 1946. *Courtesy of Photographic Archives, Appalachian Learning Laboratory, Alice Lloyd College*

James Brandenburg, Estill County, serving in World War II. *Courtesy of Wilma Osborne Hamilton*

Samuel L. Hamilton serving in the Navy, 1944. He was called into service three days before graduating from high school so missed his graduation ceremony. *Courtesy of Mary Hamilton Adams*

Perry County Courthouse, Main Street, Hazard, circa 1945. This building stood from 1912 to 1964. *Courtesy of Bobby Davis Museum and Park*

Stuffley Knob fire tower was constructed in the Big Sandy Unit by the Kentucky Division of Forestry in 1947. It was located between Little Paint Creek, Asa Creek and Barnetts Creek. Ranger E. H. Price is in the foreground with his Division of Forestry truck by the tower. *Courtesy of Winifred "Wini" Berckman Humphrey*

Railroad car loaded with evaporated milk from Hazard, Feb. 26, 1948. The milk drive was sponsored by the Junior Chamber of Commerce of Hazard and was sent to Europe. *Courtesy of Photographic Archives, Appalachian Learning Laboratory, Alice Lloyd College*

Pikeville Methodist Hospital Board of Trustees, 1949. Included: R. G. Wells, Rev. John W. Worthington, Rev. Robert L. Anderson, John A. McCown, F. S. Huffman, Frank Harrison, Elster Ratliff, W. P. Fryman, Joseph D. Darkins, F. H. Rice, Mrs. Conrad B. Rice, R. W. Gibson, Mrs. J. E. Johnson, C. M. Caudill, Rev. Frank Hopkins, Frank C. King, Rev. W. H. Smith, W. P. Davis, C. W. Krebs, Mrs. John DuPuy, C. V. Snapp, K. J. Day, P. B. Stratton. Ex-Officio: Dr. G. R. Tomlin, Dr. Paul C. Gillespie, Dr. R. R. Patton, Dr. A. R. Perkins, Dr. Carl E. Vogel and Dr. F. D. Rose. *Courtesy of Pikeville Medical Center*

Hospital Guild at Pikeville Methodist Hospital, 1949. Included: Mrs. Vernon Stump, Mrs. K. J. Day, Mrs. Martha Barrett, Mrs. E. L. Howerton, Rev. and Mrs. Thomas B. Ashley, Rev. and Mrs. John W. Worthington, Rev. and Mrs. H. Driskell, Mrs. F. T. Doepel, Mrs. Dixie Ratliff, Mrs. H. D. Calhoun, Mrs. Dewey Johnson, Miss Kathleen West, Mrs. Felix Compton, Mrs. L. H. Whitman, Mrs. F. L. Rice, Mrs. James Sowards, Mrs. Virginia Redman, Mrs. J. B. Goff, Mrs. A. S. Corbin, Miss Virginia West, Mrs. Pearl Lemon, Mrs. C. R. Brown, Mrs. W. T. Huffman Jr., Mrs. J. H. Fisher, Mrs. John McCown, Mrs. C. M. Sullivan, Mrs. Laura Ford, Miss Mary Baker, Mrs. Naomi Ladson, Mrs. J. L. Morgan, Mrs. D. T. Keel, Mrs. T. C. Guthrie, Mrs. W. L. Mize, Mrs. Nora Cox, Wanda Jean Skiles, Mrs. George Pinson Jr. and Mrs. A. T. Ratliff. *Courtesy of Pikeville Medical Center*

Middlesboro Police Department, March 1949. Seated are George Ridings and Guy Herrell. Standing, left to right: Ernest Mike, Bill Shoffner, Cecil Grubbs, Joseph Evans, Mike Shumate, Herman Welch, Boyd Webb, Dewey Dillman, Bill Moody, Sam Brown, Elmer Sowder, George Shelton and John Dixon. *Courtesy of Bell County Historical Society*

Police confiscating a still in Middlesboro. *Courtesy of Bell County Historical Society*

Hazard Fire Department trucks, circa 1950. *Courtesy of Photographic Archives, Appalachian Learning Laboratory, Alice Lloyd College*

Kentucky State Police officers in Hazard, circa 1955. *Courtesy of Photographic Archives, Appalachian Learning Laboratory, Alice Lloyd College*

Political rally in Hindman, circa 1958. Norman Cornett is holding his daughter, Lisa, in front on the street. *Courtesy of Kimberly C. Brashear*

Middlesboro Fire Department in front of City Hall, circa 1955. From left to right: Bill Moody, Dewey Dillman, Walter "Shorty" Venable, Jim Harrell, Ted Yeary, unidentified, fire chief Richard Knipp, George Owens and Bebe Green. *Courtesy of Bell County Historical Society*

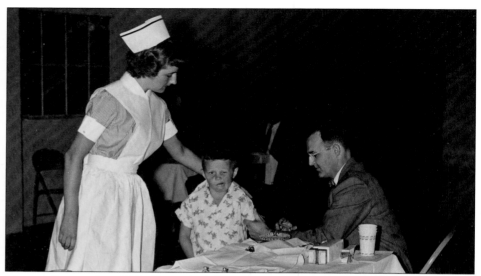

Lewis Frank Fowler and his sister, Shelby Ann, at McKee in Jackson County, circa 1955. Lewis served in the Korean Conflict. *Courtesy of Wilma Osborne Hamilton*

Lucien H. Rice, SP5, U.S. Army, October 1956. He served from 1956 to 1959. *Courtesy of Lucien H. Rice*

First polio vaccine clinic, Berea Public School, May 2, 1955. Betty Cuderson is the nurse helping Dr. Norman C. Wheeler. Dr. J. W. Armstrong and Dr. Eugene Parr are in the background. *Courtesy of Appalachian Photoarchives, Southern Appalachian Archives, Berea College*

Bill Gorman, left, and Vernon Cooper meet on Main Street in Hazard before the groundbreaking of Buckhorn Dam, 1956. *Courtesy of Bobby Davis Museum and Park*

Kentucky Division of Forestry Fire School at Pineville, 1956. Kneeling, left to right: Harry Nadler, Walter N. Green, A. L. Sturdivant and Harrod B. Newland. Standing: Gene L. Butcher, H. W. Berckman, Maynard Marcum, Robert F. Collins, John Keetuh and Frank Hood. *Courtesy of Winifred "Wini" Berckman Humphrey*

Frontier nurse Anna Mae January visits a home on Hurricane Creek near its confluence with the Middle Fork of the Kentucky River, circa 1955. *Courtesy of Appalachian Photoarchives, Southern Appalachian Archives, Berea College*

Pikeville Methodist Hospital, circa 1960. *Courtesy of Pikeville Medical Center*

Nursing students at Pikeville Methodist Hospital, 1962. *Courtesy of Pikeville Medical Center*

Middlesboro Police Department, circa 1960. Front row, left to right: Buster Williams, Tommy Grey, Cecil Grubbs, chief George Ridings and Elmer Wyatt. Second row: James Pursifull, Charles Fretwell, Bill Shumate, John Bunch and Verlin Thompson. Back row: Don Webb, Walter Turner, T. S. Siler, Doug Campbell and James Evans. *Courtesy of Bell County Historical Society*

President Lyndon B. Johnson squats on the porch beside Tom Fletcher, age 38, and two of his eight children at Inez, April 24, 1964. Johnson was visiting Eastern Kentucky on a "poverty tour." Fletcher told Johnson he'd been out of work almost two years and had earned only $400 in all of 1963. *Courtesy of Photographic Archives, Appalachian Learning Laboratory, Alice Lloyd College*

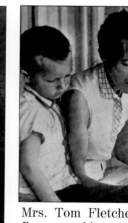

Mrs. Tom Fletcher with her five-year-old son, Alvin, reading letters sent from people after Lyndon B. Johnson visited their home in Inez on his "poverty tour," May 15, 1964. *Courtesy of Photographic Archives, Appalachian Learning Laboratory, Alice Lloyd College*

U.S. senator and presidential candidate Robert Kennedy on Liberty Street in Hazard during his 1968 visit to Appalachia. *Courtesy of Appalachian Photoarchives, Southern Appalachian Archives, Berea College*

Pikeville Methodist Hospital Board of Directors, July 1969, left to right: C. V. Snapp, Walter May, Buddy Johnson, Elmer Blackburn, Lon Rogers, Walter P. Walters, Lee Keene, W. Ernest Elliott, Vivian Day, J. I. Meyer, E. Bruce Walters and Ed Elder. *Courtesy of Pikeville Medical Center*

Construction underway for the new Elliott Building of the Pikeville Methodist Hospital, 1969. *Courtesy of Pikeville Medical Center*

DISASTERS

Perhaps the most dramatic natural disaster ever to hit Eastern Kentucky came along 300 million years ago, when an asteroid crashed into what is now Bell County, creating a large round depression where the town of Middlesboro now sits.

In more modern times, disasters — not counting those in which coal miners are trapped underground — almost always mean floods and fires.

The floods come with the geography. A region created largely by the erosion of the Cumberland Plateau has many creeks and rivers winding through narrow valleys, and the only naturally flat lands often are in flood plains. Mix in a heavy rain and the result is water in homes and businesses, followed by a muddy mess.

The most widespread flooding in the period covered by this book was in 1957 and 1963. But there were great floods across the region before that period and after. Even today mountain residents whose homes are cheek by jowl with a flashy creek sleep with one eye open when there is too much rain hitting the roof.

Aftermath of the flood of 1957 on the west side of Main Street in Hazard. *Courtesy of Bobby Davis Museum and Park*

Fire on Railroad Street, Morehead, circa 1945. *Courtesy of Camden-Carroll Library, Morehead State University, Roger W. Barbour Collection*

Fire at the Pikeville Elementary School and gymnasium, 1947. *Courtesy of Ann E. Carty*

Ohio River flood at Catlettsburg, January 1950. *Courtesy of Frank Godbey and Margaret Godbey Braun*

South Jackson under water, Feb. 14, 1948. *Courtesy of Kathy Carter*

Cleaning up the schools after Pikeville was flooded in 1957. *Courtesy of Ann E. Carty*

1957 flood in Hazard. *Courtesy of Bobby Davis Museum and Park*

Sam Owada surveying the 1957 flood damage to Kelemen's restaurant, Modern Cafe, in Cumberland. *Courtesy of Sam Owada*

Virginia Theater fire on Main Street, Hazard, 1962. The theater is down the street beyond the cars on the left. *Courtesy of Bobby Davis Museum and Park*

Middlesboro flood, 1963. *Courtesy of Bell County Historical Society*

Flood damage at Harlan, March 13, 1963. *Courtesy of Photographic Archives, Appalachian Learning Laboratory, Alice Lloyd College*

Kentucky Street in Harlan after the flood, March 13, 1963. *Courtesy of Photographic Archives, Appalachian Learning Laboratory, Alice Lloyd College*

Chester Stevens on Main Street, Hazard, during the flood of 1963. The J. J. Newberry Department Store shows the water level. *Courtesy of Bobby Davis Museum and Park*

Hazard flood, March 1963, looking from Baker Hill north toward the Hibler Hotel at the right center. To the left of the hotel is Halcomb's Shoe Store. Town Bridge is in the background. The river reached 37 feet which was two feet short of the 1957 flood crest. *Courtesy of Bobby Davis Museum and Park*

Main Street, Hazard, 1963. The man on the left in the white coat is Chester Stevens. Bill Minor is talking to a man in the center of the street. *Courtesy of Bobby Davis Museum and Park*

Fire at Delbert Hopkin's Cafe, Pine Street in Pineville, circa 1963. *Courtesy of Bell County Historical Society*

G. Garston Building on fire, Middlesboro, circa 1964. *Courtesy of Bell County Historical Society*

COMMERCE & INDUSTRY

Eastern Kentucky has been blessed with the world's oldest and most diverse forest, and some of its thickest and most extensive coal seams. Those have formed the backbone of the region's commerce and industry, and forced cycles of fat and lean times.

Many people worked for the coal company and spent their money — or script — in the company store. But no matter what you did for a living, your well-being and that of those around you was largely dependent on the price of coal and lumber.

By 1940, the labor conflicts that had led to one county becoming nationally known as "Bloody Harlan" had subsided somewhat, and the United Mine Workers became a force that coal operators had to deal with.

Historians point out that the greatest long-term threat facing miners was modern equipment.

In 1950, nearly 67,000 coal miners were employed in Kentucky, mostly in the Eastern Kentucky coal fields. By 1965, that number had decreased to 20,000, but each miner was producing far more coal.

Downtown Pikeville, circa 1950. *Courtesy of Pikeville Public Library, Paul B. Mays Collection*

Yancy, circa 1940, was founded in 1918 by Elzo and Elbert Guthrie on Slater's Branch of Catrons Creek five miles southeast of Harlan. It had about 1,000 people, a post office, commissary, movie house, doctor's office, school and churches. Silk stocking row, on the right, housed the owners and management staff and families. Most of the people lived on the mountain to the left and behind the tipple on that part of the mountain. There was an explosion in 1932 killing 23 men. *Courtesy of Paul F. Guthrie*

Latiff Food Market, Middlesboro. *Courtesy of Bell County Historical Society*

Renfro Valley Barn Dances drew a crowd, circa 1940. *Courtesy of Appalachian Photoarchives, Southern Appalachian Archives, Berea College*

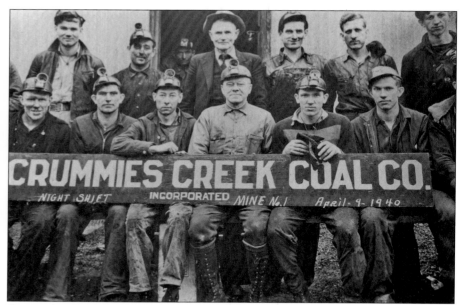

Inland Steel Company of Wheelwright, circa 1940. Front row, left to right: G. C. Billips, mine foreman; E. R. Price, superintendent; William G. Fletcher, general superintendent; and F. B. Blackburn, night foreman. Back row: Blaine Smith, chief clerk; J. C. Osborne, chief electrician; H. M. Wilkinson, store manager; G. C. Sutherland, safety engineer; J. W. Bailey, physician; J. T. Parker, assistant superintendent; and H. O. Zimmerman, chief engineer. *Courtesy of Nancy Bailey Griffin*

Crummies Creek Coal Mine No. 1 employees in Harlan County, 1940. William Coldiron is second from the right in the last row. *Courtesy of Sarah Coldiron Camden*

United Mine Workers of America union gathering on Main Street in Cumberland, circa 1940. Hamp C. Wooten Sr. is kneeling in front with the black suit with a badge. *Courtesy of Beuna Wooten*

John A. Webb, without the hat, and his daughters, Mae and Dixie, in the Webbs' fashionable clothing store in Whitesburg, circa 1942. *Courtesy of Dale Wilson*

Park Theater and Bus Depot in Middlesboro, 1946. *Courtesy of Bell County Historical Society*

Cumberland Avenue, Middlesboro, circa 1945. *Courtesy of Bell County Historical Society*

Pikeville Livestock Market, 1944. *Courtesy of Pikeville Public Library, Paul B. Mays Collection*

Battson's Beauty Bar, Morehead, circa 1945. *Courtesy of Camden-Carroll Library, Morehead State University, Roger W. Barbour Collection*

Kentucky Power Company employees, 1944. Front row, left to right: Shode (unknown), Everett (unknown), Billy (unknown), Moscoe Blackburn and Roy (unknown). Back row: Ron (unknown), Logan (unknown), Rae (unknown), Louey (unknown), B. K. E. and Fred Barnett. *Courtesy of Vickie Blackburn*

Ray Lytle store, Morehead, circa 1945. *Courtesy of Camden-Carroll Library, Morehead State University, Roger W. Barbour Collection*

Shoppers inside the Big Jim Coal Co. store at Blanche in Bell County, Sept. 4, 1946. *Courtesy of Photographic Archives, Appalachian Learning Laboratory, Alice Lloyd College*

Men take the oath as they join the local United Mine Workers union at Black Mountain Coal Co. 30-31 Mine, Harlan County, Sept. 8, 1946. The meeting was held in a church. *Courtesy of Photographic Archives, Appalachian Learning Laboratory, Alice Lloyd College*

Theater on Wilson Avenue, Morehead, 1944. *Courtesy of Camden-Carroll Library, Morehead State University, Roger W. Barbour Collection*

General store operated by a subsidiary company, U.S. Coal & Coke Co., U.S. 30 and 31 Mines, Lynch, Harlan County, Sept. 19, 1946. *Courtesy of Photographic Archives, Appalachian Learning Laboratory, Alice Lloyd College*

Kentucky Utilities linemen banquet celebration at the home of Earl and Gertrude Ward, Calloway, the day they turned power on the new lines from Blackmont to the top of Tan Yard Hill, circa 1946. Earl Ward and Speed Campbell were instrumental in getting people to sign deeds on the grounds where the post holes were dug. When necessary, they volunteered to see that all homes were wired in order to make the overall project successful. *Courtesy of Bell County Historical Society*

Kentucky Power Company crew, 1946, left to right: Eugene (unknown), Clarence (unknown), John (unknown), Jess (unknown), Shug (unknown), Ernie (unknown), Mack (unknown) and Fred (unknown). *Courtesy of Vickie Blackburn*

Major's Department Store in Hazard, 1948. *Courtesy of Bobby Davis Museum and Park*

Main Street of Jackson, 1948. *Courtesy of Kathy Carter*

Downtown Pikeville, circa 1950. *Courtesy of Pikeville Public Library, Paul B. Mays Collection*

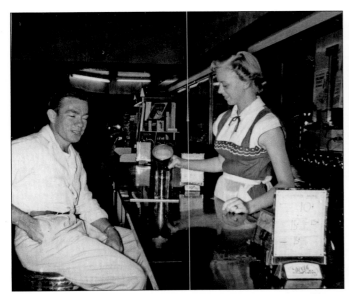

Jim Leach and Betty Jane Crawford at Bishop Drug Store at the corner of Main and South Wilson streets, Morehead, circa 1950. *Courtesy of Cindy Leach*

Clyde Osborne and his crew sawing at the mill just out of South Irvine on Wagersville Road, circa 1950. *Courtesy of Wilma Osborne Hamilton*

Liquor store in Middlesboro before the county went dry. *Courtesy of Bell County Historical Society*

Banquet at Louie's Cafe, Pikeville, circa 1950. *Courtesy of Pikeville Public Library, Paul B. Mays Collection*

Workers in Lee Clay Products Co., Clearfield, 1951. Lee Clay Products was established by A. W. Lee and John W. Wrigley of Clearfield, Pennsylvania. Their company purchased the assets of the Clearfield Lumber Company, and engineers employed Martin Bowne to decide what else could be done with the land the company owned. He discovered the area was mostly clay and ideal for sewage and drain pipes and septic tanks. In 1921 the Clearfield Lumber Company was torn down and in its place was built a tile plant complete with machinery to cast the flint and plastic clay for baking and curing in coal-fired kilns. Lee Clay started production in 1923 and prospered from the beginning. The clay in the area was so much better quality than could be found elsewhere and was shipped around the country. The plant stayed open through the Depression avoiding layoffs by splitting the work with each man getting three days of work a week. Lee Clay was the last coal-burning clay plant in the United States, closing in November 1970. *Courtesy of Rowan County Public Library*

Main Street of Hazard, 1948. *Courtesy of Bobby Davis Museum and Park*

Inside Liberty Coal Company in Hyden, Leslie County, 1954. The man on the left is an insurance salesman selling health plans to the miners. His partner took the photograph. The mine foreman gave permission for the salesmen to walk into the mines to present their plans. The bonus to the miners was to receive a free photograph of their visit. This was special since not many families in the area owned cameras at that time. The miner on the right is Edwin Anderson who worked for 31 years in the coal mines. *Courtesy of Phillip B. Anderson*

Cutting crew inside Liberty Coal Company in Hyden, Leslie County, 1954. The crew is using a cutting saw to prepare the coal for removal. The saw, with a blade like a horizontal chain saw, is used to cut several lateral cuts in the coal seams in the mine, then the coal could be removed. The man in the clean clothes on the left is an insurance salesmen trying to sell the miners health insurance plans. *Courtesy of Phillip B. Anderson*

First National Bank, Pikeville, 1954. *Courtesy of Pikeville Public Library, Paul B. Mays Collection*

Looking down Main Street in Hazard, circa 1955. *Courtesy of Photographic Archives, Appalachian Learning Laboratory, Alice Lloyd College*

H&P Supermarket, Hazard, circa 1955. *Courtesy of Bobby Davis Museum and Park*

Teach Sloane and his son at a small seam coal mine near Pippa Passes, circa 1955. *Courtesy of Appalachian Photoarchives, Southern Appalachian Archives, Berea College*

Gas rig on Combs Branch at Dwarf, circa 1955. Earl Fugate is on the left. *Courtesy of Joyce Smith*

Hamp C. Wooten Sr., circa 1955. He was a miner that drove the Joy Loader for United States Steel Corporation, Lynch Mines. *Courtesy of Beuna Wooten*

Cumberland Avenue, Middlesboro, circa 1955. *Courtesy of Bell County Historical Society*

F. W Woolworth Co., Middlesboro, circa 1955. *Courtesy of Bell County Historical Society*

Newt Hylton and his son, Albert, pitch a stack of hay on Laurel Fork Creek, circa 1955. *Courtesy of Appalachian Photoarchives, Southern Appalachian Archives, Berea College*

White Lumber Co., Morehead, 1956. *Courtesy of Rowan County Public Library*

Street in Hazard decorated for Christmas, circa 1957. *Courtesy of Photographic Archives, Appalachian Learning Laboratory, Alice Lloyd College*

Mrs. Imal Trout behind the counter at Radwins Shoe Store, Pikeville, circa 1960. *Courtesy of Pikeville Public Library, Paul B. Mays Collection*

Downtown Middlesboro businesses, circa 1960. *Courtesy of Bell County Historical Society*

Hotel Cumberland, Middlesboro, circa 1960. *Courtesy of Bell County Historical Society*

Looking at a coal seam inside old No. 1 mine owned by the Pocahontas Fuel Co. at Harlan, Jan. 31, 1960. After the mine was worked out, it was converted to an exhibition that could be driven through. *Courtesy of Photographic Archives, Appalachian Learning Laboratory, Alice Lloyd College*

Sidewalk Sale in Middlesboro, 1962. *Courtesy of Bell County Historical Society*

First National Bank of Middlesboro, circa 1964. *Courtesy of Bell County Historical Society*

Salesman Keith Soper from Lee Clay Products Co. with Bill Minor, People's Lumber, Lothair, circa 1962. *Courtesy of Rowan County Public Library*

Moscoe Blackburn's Kentucky Power Company crew with the mule, Big Red, who was used to pull the power poles up the mountain to install the power by Buckhorn Lake when the lake was being built, 1966. John "Big John" Pennington is beside Big Red. The other three men are Crusoe Holiday, A. Bryant and Herschel Adams. *Courtesy of Vickie Blackburn*

TRANSPORTATION

Horses and mules still were an important part of the transportation picture in the mountains in 1940. By the 1970s, however, the automobile had taken over.

Service stations, with signs that said "Gulf" or "Standard Oil," became a common fixture in every town. The cars themselves went through design changes that saw the rise and fall of tail fins.

Most towns also had a bus station. The railroad also was important. It employed many people, shuttled passengers everywhere and, of course, carried the coal to market.

A great but little-known story is found in the caption below one of the photos in this section: A woman wins a car — a brand-new 1947 Hudson, no less — in a newspaper subscription contest. Then she takes it home and her daughter, backing out of the driveway, turns the wheel the wrong way and flips it into a creek.

The gondolas, as the railroad cars were called, looking across the North Fork of the Kentucky River and North Main Street in Hazard, circa 1946. The large three-story building on the right is the YMCA. Note the variation in the size of coal in the gondolas. Coal could be ordered in different sizes depending on its purpose. *Courtesy of Bobby Davis Museum and Park*

Service station owned by Jack Helwig, Morehead, circa 1945. *Courtesy of Camden-Carroll Library, Morehead State University, Roger W. Barbour Collection*

Railroad Depot, Morehead, circa 1945. *Courtesy of Camden-Carroll Library, Morehead State University, Roger W. Barbour Collection*

Vernon Alfrey's filling station on U.S. Highway 60 in Morehead, circa 1945. *Courtesy of Camden-Carroll Library, Morehead State University, Roger W. Barbour Collection*

Greyhound Restaurant and bus station in Morehead, circa 1945. *Courtesy of Camden-Carroll Library, Morehead State University, Roger W. Barbour Collection*

L & N Railroad truck and workers. *Courtesy of Bell County Historical Society*

L & N Railroad workers, circa 1945. Second from the left is Isaac Little from Hazard. *Courtesy of Vickie Blackburn*

This 1947 Hudson from Calverts automobile dealership in Morehead was won by Mrs. Lyde Carter of Christy Creek. She won the blue four-door automobile by selling the most subscriptions to the Rowan County News. The contestants, left to right: Sara Elam, Earl Wood or Versie Hamm, unidentified, Thelma Brenham, Merl Gregory and Lyde Carter. Standing in the doorway are John Michael Praitt, left, and Muruel Bradley. Shortly after taking the car home, the Carter's daughter, Lois Ann, turned the car over into the creek while backing out of the driveway. *Courtesy of Camden-Carroll Library, Morehead State University, Roger W. Barbour Collection*

C & O Railroad station at Pikeville, 1946. *Courtesy of Pikeville Public Library, Paul B. Mays Collection*

Mule hitched to a sled on a morning with light snow at the Fields Farm, Lost Creek, Breathitt County, 1948. From left to right: Rev. Henry Clay Fields, local missionary worker Miss Bethke, Rev. Ray Fields with wife Mary Lopp Fields and Rev. Henry's wife, Sally Fields. *Courtesy of Carol Fields Shepherd*

Henry H. Curtright with the hearse from Curtright Funeral Home, February 1948. Curtright founded the business in 1927, providing the first licensed funeral director and embalmer, the first motor equipment, the first factory-made caskets and the first ambulance service in Louisa and Lawrence counties. *Courtesy of Linda Fugitt*

U.S. Highway 23 South before the cut-thru, Pikeville, 1946. *Courtesy of Pikeville Public Library, Paul B. Mays Collection*

The Louisville & Nashville Railroad employees gathered in London in 1950. They had completed a course in "Living Better," part of the railroad's industrial education program. The L & N was a leading employer in Southeastern Kentucky, providing freight hauling for coal and passenger service connections to the nation's railway network. *Courtesy of John M. Shotwell*

Transporting clay by rail at Lee Clay Products Co., 1951. *Courtesy of Rowan County Public Library*

Chesapeake & Ohio Railway Limeville pusher engine in Greenup County, July 1951. The engine pushed coal trains up the grade to the northern bridge over the Ohio River on their way to Lake Erie. From left to right: conductor R. H. Smith, fireman T. S. Truitt, coaler V. Traylor, coaler A. Roten and engineer Isaiah Clark Sandy. *Courtesy of Michael Wells*

Cars in Colwell's used car lot on the corner in Hazard, circa 1958. *Courtesy of Photographic Archives, Appalachian Learning Laboratory, Alice Lloyd College*

Car show at the Hazard school gymnasium, circa 1954. *Courtesy of Photographic Archives, Appalachian Learning Laboratory, Alice Lloyd College*

Thelma Seale getting into her father's Buick in front of his service station in Cawood, 1959. *Courtesy of T. J. Seale*

Rev. Henry C. and Sally Fields riding Old Maud to Big Branch Church in Breathitt County, circa 1952. *Courtesy of Carol Fields Shepherd*

Cars parked across from the Standard Oil service station on East Main Street in Hazard, circa 1960. The construction to the left of the service station is the Woodland Restaurant, part of the Woodland Motel. *Courtesy of Photographic Archives, Appalachian Learning Laboratory, Alice Lloyd College*

SPORTS & LEISURE

Eastern Kentuckians have always loved their local sports teams. It seems that everyone knows the names of players on the high school basketball or football team, especially if the team is winning games and advancing in tournament play.

Fans' interest can reach a fever pitch when the scrappy mountain team advances to competition on the state level, particularly if a team of flatlanders is vanquished. In this section, you will find two photos of the Breckinridge Training High School from Morehead, which beat Dawson Spring 68-36 for the 1946 state basketball championship. Such victories usually were followed by the whole town — the whole county — turning out to welcome the conquering heroes.

Quite often, the fan adulation carried on to professional teams that once were found in Eastern Kentucky. Here you will find images of the Hazard Bombers and the Middlesboro Senators.

Also check out the photo of people playing slot machines — yes, slot machines! — in Middlesboro in the years when such devices, and alcohol sales, were legal there.

Red Cross senior life saving class at Bobby Davis pool, 1947. Front row, left to right: Roland Combs, unidentified, Buddy Beadles, Sonny Gumm, John E. Bowling, unidentified, Paul Townes, unidentified and Lillian Seamon. Back row: Charles Luttrell, Robert Lee Marks, (unknown) Ward, Kenny Gilbert, Arnold Gene Feltner, unidentified, Tom Turke, unidentified, Betty Carson, Jack Gazay and Bill Davis. *Courtesy of Bobby Davis Museum and Park*

Flatwoods Eagles baseball team, circa 1940. Team members: manager Ralph Phelps, Sidney Miller, Athel Wyant, Tom Lewis, Chester Keiser, Earl Williams, Herbert Meade, Tom Wilson, Edward Powell, Art KcAKee, Homer Strother, George Potters, Carman McKenzie, John Conlon and Lester Tackett. *Courtesy of Bonnie Phelps Sweatman*

Hardburly Coal Co. basketball team, 1940. *Courtesy of Bobby Davis Museum and Park*

Middlesboro Athletics, Class D baseball. Left to right: Floyd Ball, Bob Bowman and Ted Russ. Ted Russ married Benny Jo Hurst at home plate in Hilltop Park. *Courtesy of Bell County Historical Society*

Pikeville High School basketball team, 1941. Front row, left to right: Denzel Hamilton, Harold Mullins, Bruce Elliott, George Venters, Marley Newsom holding team mascot Tootsie, Clem Wiser and Chester Elswick. Back row: manager Cody White, Anderson Ridenour, Estill Ishmael, Clarence Damron, Tom Bales, Woodrow Coleman and Coach Hatcher. *Courtesy of Ann E. Carty*

Football team from Pikeville High School, 1942. Front row, left to right: Paul Blair, Paul Shaw, James Bloomer, unidentified, Clyde Hobson, Henry Stratton, Marley Newsom, Junior Goodson, Robert Dyer and C. D. Roberts. Second row: unidentified, unidentified, Grover Justice, James Serginnis, Chester Elswick, Ralph Goff and John Sowards. Third row: unidentified, unidentified, John Thomas Blackburn, unidentified, unidentified, Tom Ashley, Tom Black, Arnold Kelley, unidentified, Hubert Vanover, manager Larry Keathley and coach "Cack" Hatcher.

Courtesy of Ann E. Carty

Navy V-12 program basketball team at Berea College, circa 1944. *Courtesy of Appalachian Photoarchives, Southern Appalachian Archives, Berea College*

Morehead High School basketball team and cheerleaders, circa 1945. *Courtesy of Camden-Carroll Library, Morehead State University, Roger W. Barbour Collection*

Football players from Hazard, 1946. *Courtesy of Bobby Davis Museum and Park*

Breckinridge Training High School basketball state champions, 1946. Front row, left to right: manager Jimmie Leach, Bill Fraley, Don Battson, Dickie Scroggins and Fred Bayes. Back row: coach Bobby Laughlin, Bill Litton, John "Sonny" Allen, Marv Mayhall, Frank Fraley, Billy Vaughn and Clayton Scaggs. *Courtesy of Cindy Leach*

Jack Parkinson, Gladys Ball, Hugh Shannon, Alva Ball, Wallace "Wah Wah" Jones and probably "Wah Wah's" mother. "Wah Wah" married Alvey and Gladys's daughter, Edna. "Wah Wah" Jones, born in Harlan in 1926, was the starting forward on the University of Kentucky's "Fabulous Five" and helped the school win NCAA national championships in 1948 and 1949.

He was also a member of the 1948 U.S. Olympic team that won the gold medal and was named an All-American in 1949. An all-around athlete, Jones also played on UK's baseball and football teams and is the only UK athlete to have his jersey retired in both football and basketball. *Courtesy of Bell County Historical Society*

Pikeville football team on Fiddlers Field, 1947. Player #48 is James "Shack" Thompson, #35 is Ervin Puitt and #38 is Don Bales. *Courtesy of Pikeville Public Library, Paul B. Mays Collection*

Advance School basketball team, Flatwoods, coached by Ralph Phelps, 1949. *Courtesy of Betty Sharp*

June Conn School of Dance, 1948, Dancers, from left to right: unidentified, "Brownie" Rogers, (unknown) Forsythe, Susan Allen, Emily Poe Walters, Judy Baker and Dura Anne Phillips. *Courtesy of Pikeville Public Library, Paul B. Mays Collection*

Benham High School football team, 1947–48. Front row, left to right: Ralph Cox, Kenneth Dixon, John D. Foutch, Bobby Guinn and Curtis Cummings. Back row: coach Charlie Davis, Walter Kilgore, Kenneth Barton, Bill Cannon, R. C. Marsh, Alan Huddleston and manager Wade Ketron. *Courtesy of anonymous*

Swimmers at the pool in Bobby Davis Park, Hazard, circa 1949. The bath house is on the right. *Courtesy of Bobby Davis Museum and Park*

Pikeville High School football team, 1949. Front row, left to right: Clark Ray Ratcliffe, Charlie Huffman, Robert Butcher, Joe Black, G. A. Campbell, Frank Justice, Robert Staggs and Bill Davidson. Second row: Dan Penny, Jim Hardman, Paul Prater, Bobby Braid, Foster Thompson, Foster York and Tracy Burke. Third row: Hallard Chaffins, Joe Steel, Howard Blackburn, Marrs May, Cecil Banks, Joe Stone and Hershel Clark. Fourth row: W. Weddington, Bill Huffman, Jim Sexton, Jim McGee, Howard Cline, Bobby Charles and Bobby Phillips. Back row: Paul Blake Adkins, assistant coach Bill Mack, unidentified, unidentified, unidentified, Andy Lorentzson and Henry Ratcliffe. *Courtesy of William G. Wheeler MD*

Community softball team, Greenup, 1950. The team was sponsored by the local department store, Mocabee's. Front row, left to right: Ray Wells, Kenneth Archey, Robert Hieneman, Cleo Garthee and Leslie Moore. Back row: Don Dover, Jack Smith, Bill Hieneman, Evert Cleary Jr., Edward Cox and Walter Willis. *Courtesy of Michael Wells*

Pikeville High School football team, 1950. Left to right: William G. Wheeler, Paul Prater, Clark Ray Ratcliffe, Marrs Allen May, Foster Thompson, Jim Sexton and Paul Blake Adkins. Back row: Joe Black, Robert Staggs, Dan Penney and Bobby Phillips. *Courtesy of William G. Wheeler MD*

John Bill "Bull" Trivette, Pikeville High School basketball coach for 16 years, teaching a physical education class, circa 1955. During his career his teams won 14 district, seven regional and five Christmas tournaments. He had seven teams that represented the 15th region at the Kentucky State Basketball Tournament. He was named All-Area Coach three times and voted the *Courier-Journal's* Kentucky Coach of the Year in 1957. *Courtesy of Ann E. Carty*

Varsity basketball team from Pikeville High School, 1952. Superintendent John York is on the right in back. In front of him is John Bill Trivette who coached at PHS for 16 years and took his teams to state seven times. *Courtesy of Ann E. Carty*

Fishing at Happy Hollow pond, circa 1950. *Courtesy of Bobby Davis Museum and Park*

Lothair School Folk Dancing Club performing in the Folk Dance Festival at Berea, circa 1950. From left to right: Mary Margaret Collins, Delores Combs, Betty Nichols, Patricia Jewell, Cynthia Ellen Bowling, Robert Stidham, Jane Nichols, Jimmy Hall, Mary Katherine Cole, Dickie Campbell, Patsy Sue Hall, Jimmy Sinor, Ada Pearl Jones and Delmar Combs. Approximately 250 young people representing seven states attended the festival. *Courtesy of Bobby Davis Museum and Park*

Playing the slot machines in Middlesboro. The community was known as "Little Las Vegas" or "Little Chicago" from the mid-1920s until the county went dry in 1955. *Courtesy of Bell County Historical Society*

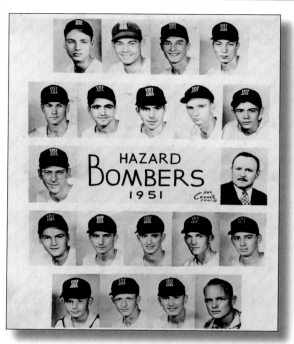

The Hazard Bombers, 1951. They were a professional baseball team for three years. On the right in the top row is Johnny Podres. He went on to pitch for the Brooklyn Dodgers, and on Oct. 4, 1955, pitched a 2-0 shutout against the New York Yankees which led to the Dodgers' win in the World Series. *Courtesy of Bobby Davis Museum and Park*

Swimland, Cumberland, circa 1952. *Courtesy of Sam Owada*

Middlesboro had the first integrated Little League team south of the Mason-Dixon Line, 1954. Front row, left to right: Billy Burch, Billy Dean, James Turner, Bobby Rogan, Roy Robinson, Danny Schultz and Kenny Williams. Back row: co-manager Monty Goforth, Lewis Wright, Richard Williams, Gary Wayne Meyers, Glenn Gooding, Johnny Spriggs, James Box, Charles Watkins and co-manager Albert Rosenbalm. *Courtesy of Bell County Historical Society*

Kentucky Power Company baseball team, 1952. Seated in the front, left to right: Earl (unknown), Russell Compton, unidentified, Gary (unknown), Adrian Combs, Moscoe Blackburn and Edgar (unknown). Standing: Jimmie O'Zee, Walter Combs, Earl Smith, Glen Logan, Everette Bush, Oscar Hudson, Arnett Strong, Bob Trent and Russell Muncy. *Courtesy of Vickie Blackburn*

Barbourville High School basketball team and cheerleaders, 1953-54. In the front, cheerleaders, left to right: Norma Jo Collier, Patsy Williamson, Betty Ann Collier, Jackie Partin, Mary Clenens Tye and Evelyn McVey. Back row: coach Herb Tye, manager Frank Disney, manager Billy Ray Lawson, Herman Playforth, Arvil Frazier, Roy Gene Woolum, Randall Coone, Hobert "Bones" Creasy, Ray Vallance, E. J. Lundy, Cookie Smith, Don Buchanon, Ray "Smoochy" Blair Canady, Gene "Shorty" Burgess, Leroy McNeil, assistant coach Jack Walker and superintendent R. H. Playforth. *Courtesy of Pat and Don Dampier*

Panthers football team, Pikeville High School, 1955. Included: Bill Scott, Jimmy Leslie, David Elliott, James Coleman, Michael Yarus, Billy Hugh Hutchinson, Tommy Charles, Max Butcher, line coach Bill Mack, Larry Phillips, Everett Justice, Larry Scott, Butch Wood, Bobby Cyrus, H. L. Justice, Robert Ratlifff and Carl Thorness. They were coached by Clayton Powers and were undefeated that year. *Courtesy of Barbara Coleman*

Pikeville Panthers basketball team, 1955-56. Front row, left to right: Buddy Elkins, James Coleman, Larry Phillips, Raleigh Wright, Lloyd Keene, Tommy Adkins and coach John Bill Trivette. Back row: manager Tommy Adkins, Wayne Rutherford, Howard Lockhart, Bill Scott, Darwin Smith, H. Justice and Joel Allen. *Courtesy of Barbara Coleman*

Barbourville High School friends on an outing to Cumberland Falls beach, June 21, 1955. One of the students was leaving for the Naval Academy in a few days. *Courtesy of Pat and Don Dampier*

Middlesboro High School 1955 football team. *Courtesy of Bell County Historical Society*

Walkertown Elementary School cheerleaders, 1956. The mascots are Regina, in the black jumper, and Vickie Blackburn in the lighter jumper. *Courtesy of Vickie Blackburn*

Hazard High School basketball team, 1957-58. *Courtesy of Vickie Blackburn*

Middlesboro High School basketball team, 1957-58. From left to right: manager Bobby Joe Smith, Doyle Milligan, Danny Schultz, Ralph Price, Houston Ball, Charlie Nagle, Jimmy Hurst, Bill Moody, John Loy, Carl Britton, Eddie Arnold, Walt Taylor and Lyle Mace. *Courtesy of Bell County Historical Society*

Middlesboro football team, circa 1960. Front row, left to right: Bill Buckner, unidentified, unidentified, Jimmy Barns, Joe McCauley, Joe Hamlett and Dan Hamilton. Second row: John Eddy Goins, Larry Lyon, David Cawood, Charlie N., John Conner, Arliss Clarkson and Don Yoakum. Third row: head coach David Hurst, coach Jim Summer, John Loy, Walt Taylor, Houston Ball, Wilburn Conner, Bob Buckner, Pepper Medley, Pat Greer, coach Lee White and coach Jack Carey. Back row: Mack Pratt, (unknown) England, unidentified, manager Eddie Parker, Bill Burch, manager W. O. Smith, unidentified, manager (unknown) Pace, Lyle Mace and Bill Dean. *Courtesy of Bell County Historical Society*

Hazard High School football team at the stadium in the Backwoods. In the front row, left to right: Jimmy Nunn, Gene Porter Fouts, Sam Lindon, Billy Joe Kidd, Sam Smith, Lloyd Caudill, Wallace Philon, Harlan "Junior" Davidson, Ronnie Lindon, Craig Williams and John Vermillion. Second row: David Stacy, James Stacy, Jerry Pigman, Deanie Sinor, Eddie Bellis, Ronnie Joseph, Ed Stacy, Johnny Stone, A. J. Davis and Bennie Pigman. Third row: unidentified, Tony Asbury, Roger Cecil, Alva Hollon, Kenny Tate, Lynn Pennington, Curt Duff, Ronnie Perkins, Butch Green and (unknown) Panky. Fourth row: Charles Thomas, Richard McGhee, Jack Robinson and (unknown) Francis. *Courtesy of Bobby Davis Museum and Park*

Claude Crook Jr. accepting the regional basketball trophy on behalf of Hazard High School, circa 1958. Handing Claude the trophy is Roy G. Eversole; principal H. M. Wesley is to his right. *Courtesy of Bobby Davis Museum and Park*

Middlesboro High School football players, 1960. *Courtesy of Bell County Historical Society*

Middlesboro High School football team, Southeastern Kentucky champions, 1959. *Courtesy of Bell County Historical Society*

Middlesboro Senators, a Pro Rookie League team, circa 1960. *Courtesy of Bell County Historical Society*

Roy G. Eversole Elementary football team of Hazard, circa 1960. On the right is Clifton Barnett. Front row, left to right, cheerleaders: Dix, Fisher, Turlish, Fouts, Kidd and coach Clifton Barnett. Second row: Little League football commissioner/coach Moscoe Blackburn, Standford, Rod, Huff, Collins, Stacey, Marcum, Fred Barnett, Springler, and Coach Hersel. Third row: Gabbard, Clifford, Joe Miller, O. Miller, Cornett, Campbell, Phillip Upchurch and Stout. Fourth row: McIntosh, Turner, Engle, Feltner, Morgan, Johnson, Godsey and Napier. Back row: Fitzpatrick, Billy Gorman, Sims, Bibee, Reed, Close, Marcum and Manning. *Courtesy of Vickie Blackburn*

Walkertown Elementary School football team, circa 1960. The coach is Moscoe Blackburn; next to Coach Blackburn is Bill Strong. *Courtesy of Vickie Blackburn*

Middlesboro High School football team, circa 1956. Coaches: W. W. Campbell, J. M. Taylor, Carl Martin and Charles Ward. Managers: Wayne Price, David Meyers, John Markham, Alex Thomasson and George Schneider. Front row, left to right: Joe Johns, James Branscome, Ed Ball, Mitchie Ghent, Bill Money, Winiford Collingsworth, Moody Taylor, Dickie Lyons, and Jake Rowland. Second row: Hugh Ed Howard, J. B. White, Larry Monhollon, John Taylor, Cecil England, R. L. Longsworth, Ronnie Curron, Boyd Martin and Paul Beach. Third row: Paul Thompson, Bill Honeycut, Jack Stanley, Denny Estes, David Lambdin, Rodger Massengill, Jimmy Hinel, Timothy Sowers and H. E. Uhl. Fourth row: Don Huddleston, Gene Redmond, Bill Cantrell, Bernard Beach, Ulis Buckner, Eulis Francisco, Clyde Murrell, Joe Rose and Horace Chadwell. *Courtesy of Bell County Historical Society*

Boat dock at Jenny Wiley State Park, circa 1960. The boats were made of wood, fiberglass and aluminum. The houseboats were mostly homemade using 55-gallon barrels welded together. Factory-made pontoons were just starting to show up on the docks at this point. *Courtesy of Barry Dean Martin*

Lining up for the movie "Jason and the Argonauts" at the theater in downtown Middlesboro, 1963. *Courtesy of Bell County Historical Society*

Hazard Little League football team coached by Moscoe Blackburn, 1965. *Courtesy of Vickie Blackburn*

Hazard High School basketball team, 1964. Coach Quillen is on the left; Coach Shackerford is on the right. *Courtesy of Vickie Blackburn*

Pikeville High School basketball team, 1962. *Courtesy of Pikeville Public Library, Paul B. Mays Collection*

Ironville School cheerleaders, 1969. In front is Kitty Watson. From left to right: Christy Lyons, Pam Stevens, Kathy Millard, Robin Kirk and Becky Robinson. In back is Linda Hill. *Courtesy of Betty Sharp*

EDUCATION

In the 1940s, one-room schools still were common in Eastern Kentucky, with students of all ages coming together to learn readin', 'ritin' and 'rithmetic. By the 1960s, some areas were so well-to-do that the Pikeville High School senior class was able to swing a trip to Daytona Beach.

Repeated studies and statistics have suggested that the region lags behind the nation in educational attainment, but you would not know that by looking at the faces of students peering out from the following pages. Here you will find a classroom run by a coal company in Harlan County in the mid-1940s, Hazard students posing to urge more school funding at about the same time, Pikeville High's senior class members in their robes and caps in the early '50s, and the school's Keyette Club from the mid-60s.

Younger readers might need to be told that those strange things students were learning to type on in 1965 were called "typewriters." And that the odd contraption shown in one classroom was a "wood stove."

Pikeville High School's 1956 graduating class. *Courtesy of Ann E. Carty and Patty Leslie Sowards*

Middlesboro High School, circa 1940. *Courtesy of Bell County Historical Society*

Berea Foundation School, 1940. Included from left to right: Danny Capps, Randall Williams, Glenn Ray Elkins, unidentified, Teddy Hesse, Betty May Taylor, Leonore Noll, Betty Lovelace, Wyldene Williams, Ikie Manning, Tommy Spillman and Shirley Baker. *Courtesy of Kathryn Freeman*

May Day celebration at the Berea Foundation School, 1940. *Courtesy of Kathryn Freeman*

Winifred Berckman, third grade, 1941. She attended a one-room school in Putney from primary through the fifth grade. *Courtesy of Winifred "Wini" Berckman Humphrey*

Middlesboro Yellow Jackets, 1949–50. *Courtesy of Bell County Historical Society*

Elementary student band at Pruden, circa 1941. Bobby Lambdin is sitting in front on the left; Eugene Lambdin is sixth from the right in the front. *Courtesy of Clarence Lambdin*

Robinson School, circa 1942. In the front row, Juanita Gayheart is fifth from the left. In the middle row, Rachel Campbell is second from the left and Jean Smith is seventh. *Courtesy of Photographic Archives, Appalachian Learning Laboratory, Alice Lloyd College*

Students at Bucks Branch one-room school at Martin, 1944. Mrs. Mae Flannery was their teacher. *Courtesy of Photographic Archives, Appalachian Learning Laboratory, Alice Lloyd College*

Venters School in Pike County, 1944. *Courtesy of Marsha Koller*

Girl friends at the Venters School, Elkhorn City, 1944. Included: Authelia Stewart, Betty Bartley, Anna Rae Damron, Janice Elswich, Pat Smith, Evelyn Coleman, Patti Huffman, Sue Owens, Mellie Lou Stewart, Gay Coleman and Fay Coleman. *Courtesy of Marsha Koller*

H. C. Hagan and students, Morehead, circa 1945. *Courtesy of Camden-Carroll Library, Morehead State University, Roger W. Barbour Collection*

Future Homemakers of America, Morehead, circa 1945. Their advisor was Virginia Rice. She is fourth from the right on the right side of the table on the right; her husband, W. H. Rice, is third from the right. *Courtesy of Lucien H. Rice*

Morehead State Teachers College senior group, 1945. *Courtesy of Camden-Carroll Library, Morehead State University, Roger W. Barbour Collection*

Students at the Bell County School, Sept. 4, 1946. *Courtesy of Photographic Archives, Appalachian Learning Laboratory, Alice Lloyd Colleg*

Pikeville High School Girls Social Club, 1945. Front row, left to right: Becky Ramsey, Pauline Bowles, Donna Sue Ratliff, Joan Hewlett, Betty Jean McCown and Fern Duty. Second row: Margaret Bartram, Betty Dana May, Mary Nell Rogers, Katherine Edwards, Ruth Saling, Ann Epperson, Nell Bevins and Patty Riley. *Courtesy of Ann E. Carty*

Children encouraging Hazard voters to "Vote Yes" for school funding, circa 1945. *Courtesy of Photographic Archives, Appalachian Learning Laboratory, Alice Lloyd College*

Ashland Junior College class of 1946. In 1937 the Ashland Board of Education announced it would start Ashland Junior College. In the late 1940s the school's enrollment grew to 460 with war veterans returning and taking advantage of the GI Bill. In the late 1950s AJC formed an alliance with the University of Kentucky to become a two-year branch. From there it became Ashland Community College out of the network of University of Kentucky related schools. *Courtesy of Michael Wells*

Louis Sergent, the tallest boy in a sport jacket, catches the bus that will take him into the Evarts High School where he is a freshman, Sept. 15, 1946. They are at the PV & K Coal Co., Clover Gap Mine, Lejunior, Harlan County. *Courtesy of Photographic Archives, Appalachian Learning Laboratory, Alice Lloyd College*

General Science class at Berea College Foundation School, 1946–47. *Courtesy of Kathryn Freeman*

Pikeville High School students in front of the courthouse celebrating Senior Day, 1946, left to right: Ann Epperson, Tracy Cushman and G. C. Leslie. This tradition ended in 1951 when a high-spirited senior stuffed paper pellets into his hog rifle and "wounded" a teacher's ear. *Courtesy of Ann E. Carty*

Classroom in the grade school at PV&K Coal Company, Clover Gap Mine, Lejunior, Harlan County, Sept. 15, 1946. *Courtesy of Photographic Archives, Appalachian Learning Laboratory, Alice Lloyd College*

Billie Smiddie was the drummer in the Benham High School marching band, 1947. *Courtesy of anonymous*

Easter play put on by Lynch Grade School children in the Lynch High School Auditorium, 1948. Beuna Wooten is in the middle of the rabbits with the ears standing straight up. *Courtesy of Beuna Wooten*

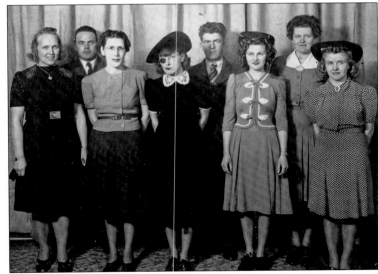

Henderson Settlement faculty, 1948, left to right: Ethel Bowlin Brown, Earl Petrey, Ruby Jones, Frances Maiden Partin, Wayland Jones, Woodie Orick Lowe, Edith Orick and Mabel Henderson Taylor. *Courtesy of Bell County Historical Society*

Sophomore girls at Middlesboro High School, 1949–50. *Courtesy of Bell County Historical Society*

Mountain Day for Berea College students, 1948. *Courtesy of Appalachian Photoarchives, Southern Appalachian Archives, Berea College*

Pikeville High School's 1949 senior class. The teacher on the left is class sponsor Rebecca Lewis who taught at PHS for 16 years; on the right is T. W. Oliver who was superintendent for 25 years. *Courtesy of Ann E. Carty*

Y-Teens, Middlesboro High School, 1949–50. *Courtesy of Bell County Historical Society*

Pikeville City School's elementary faculty, circa 1950. *Courtesy of Ann E. Carty*

Boys Glee Club, Middlesboro, 1952–53. *Courtesy of Bell County Historical Society*

First-grade teacher at McDowell for many years, Ann Tackett, with the WPA rock building and janitor's house in the background. The brown bag lunch was necessary during the 1940s and 1950s in many schools. *Courtesy of Barry Dean Martin*

Pikeville High School Class of 1952. William G. Wheeler is in the back row eighth from the right; Jim Sexton is in the fourth row on the left; Marrs Allen May is in the fourth row fourth from the left; Jim McGee is in the fourth row fifth from the right; George Eagle is in the third row on the right; Nancy Batten is in the fourth row on the right. *Courtesy of William G. Wheeler MD*

Pikeville High School band in performance on Main Street, circa 1950. The director was Herbert Pepper. *Courtesy of Ann E. Carty*

First graders, Advance School, Flatwoods, 1952–53. Top row, left to right: teacher Beverly Melvin, unidentified, Joyce Starcher, unidentified, Judy Duty, Jim Bradley, unidentified, Roger Willis and Glenda Greene. Second row: Ralph Damron, Marcheta Glazier, unidentified, unidentified, unidentified and Leslie Frasure. Third row: Sue Setzer, Phillip Haines, unidentified, unidentified, Betty Jo Argibrite, Richard Callihan, unidentified, Randy Lynch and Becky Powell. Fourth row: Ralph Dickerson, Brenda Stevens, Joe Green, Betty Phelps, unidentified, Virgil Knipp and John Whitt. *Courtesy of Betty Sharp*

Thespians at Middlesboro High School, 1953–54. Included: Juanita Massengill, Charlotte Siler, Bess Brittion, Shirley Green, Pat Turner, Neville Tucker, Barbara Brittion, Jane Beason, Billye Anne Alexander, Boyd Martin, Barbara Daniels, Dorsie Preston, Sally Wiedenhoefer, Clara Ann Tucker, Mary George Faulkner, Manny Carter, Macavley Arthur, Jackie Harrell, Dicky Lyon, Jake Rowland, Irwin Wakin, Richard Williamson, Armond Taylor and Wayne Idol. *Courtesy of Bell County Historical Society*

Junior class at Breckinridge Training School, Morehead, 1951. The students are in history class. The school was located on the grounds of Morehead University. Starting on the left, front to back: Jimmy Ewan, Betty Jane Crawford, Jean Bowan, Louella Litton and Bob Barber. The teacher is George T. Young. Second row: Lida Lou Cash, Jimmy Coleman, Barbara Scaggs and unidentified. Third row: Peggy Wood, unidentified, Clinton Holbrook, J. T. Green, Phillip Lewis and unidentified. Fourth row: Carol Sue Cash, Louise Crosswaite, Pat Crutcher, Bobby Compton, Bernard Kautz and Lucien Rice. Fifth row: Clyda Jo Wells and (unknown) Gevedon. In the back row: Margaret Vinson, Jack McBrayer, William Earl Clay, Don Bishop and Don Young. *Courtesy of Lucien H. Rice*

Hazard High School band, 1954–55. In front, left to right: James Stidham, unidentified and Buzz Wombles. First row: Fitzy Gilbert, Johnnie Jane Shackleford, Barbara Walker, Maud Shackleford, Cecelia Johnson, Tudy Gilbert, Jayne Rose Abshear, Wilna Browning and Wilberta Combs. Second row: Elizabeth York, unidentified, Bobbie Webb, unidentified, unidentified, Ann Hemphill, unidentified, Fred Copeland, David Copeland, Jimmy Crutchfield, unidentified, Linda Sammons, Jackie Petrey, Millie Baumgardner and George Luke. Third row: (unknown) Shaheen, Johnny Gabbard, Leslie Stone, Freida (unknown), Kent Combs, Jimmy Hacker, Harry Minnick, Harmon Petrey, Raleigh Johnson, Fred Stidham, Jitter Fouts, Sandra Lindon, Lloyd Browning, unidentified, Asbel Johnson, Joe Harold Shepherd, unidentified, unidentified, Charles Nicholson and Phil Davis. Back row: Linda Stevens, Harlan Stone, unidentified, Jimmy Hall, Gayle White, unidentified and Jimmy Davis with the rest unidentified until Betty Hemphill on the right. *Courtesy of Bobby Davis Museum and Park*

Students at Lees College, Jackson, 1953. From left to right: Janallee Stamper, Bobby James Ison and Bernice Stamper. *Courtesy of Janallee Mullins*

Mrs. C. E. Bunnell, a retired public school teacher, ran a small private school in her home in Corbin. This is her last graduation in May 1953 before she left teaching due to poor health. Front row, left to right: graduating second graders Wayne Donaldson, Mazie Blanton, Mrs. Bunnell, Jan Fisher and Scotty Russell. Back row: graduating first graders Clara Hart, John Shotwell, Carolyn Wainscott, Douglas Bozarth, John KcKearan, David Dunn and Fred Cox. *Courtesy of John M. Shotwell*

High School dance in the gymnasium at Pikeville High School, 1955. From left to right: James Coleman, Barbara Thompson, Lloyed Keene, Gail Coleman, Donna Stewart, Bill Clark, Max Butcher and Mickey Clark. *Courtesy of Barbara Coleman*

Senior Skip Day from Barbourville High School, 1955. They spent the day at Cumberland Falls. In front of the car, left to right: Ruth Mills, Pat Brunk and Georgia McDonald. Behind the car are Gary Martin and Kent Clark. *Courtesy of Pat and Don Dampier*

Casual class picture of the Class of 1955, Barbourville High School. The class included: Jimmy Maurice Bays, Florence Ann Prichard Blackwood, Patricia Marie Brunk, Gene A. Burgess, Marilyn Inez Buttery, Ann Faulkner Camden, Eleanor Carruth, Sammie Carter Jr., Kent Randolph Clark, Norma Jo Collier, Randall Coone, Harold Leon Disney, Patricia Ann Disney, Charlotte Geneva Douglas, Billy Farris Frederick, Charles K. Gambrel, Charles Hermon Grant, Gerald L. Hood, Jacqueline Faye Hyde, James William Jones, Ronald Wayne Lynch, Georgia Louise McDonald, Stanley Leroy McNeil, Wetzel R. McWilliams, Gary Wayne Martin, Charles Richard Matthews, Wilma Ruth Mills, Bobby J. Pickard, Roscoe Herman Playforth Jr., Margie Sue Seale, Aruthur Allan Smith, Betty Jean Taylor and Patricia Anne Williamson. *Courtesy of Pat and Don Dampier*

Middlesboro High School's annual staff, 1955. Back row, left to right: Harry Chambers, unidentified, Dickie Lyons, unidentified, Neville Ann Tucker, Jimmy Hoe, Mary Joe Faulkner, E. T. Moore, unidentified, Irvin Wakin, and Lynette Wilder. In the front row June Hurst is fifth from the left, Ellen Webb is in the dark blouse and Sally Wiedenhoefer is in the white blouse with dark trim. *Courtesy of Bell County Historical Society*

Getting a drink during recess at Hindman Settlement School, circa 1955. *Courtesy of Appalachian Photoarchives, Southern Appalachian Archives, Berea College*

Morehead Normal School reunion in Morehead, circa 1955. Included: Jimmie Bishop, Arthur Bradley, Anna Bradley, Harry Bradley, Ollie Burns, C. P. Caudill, D. B. Caudill, Etta Caudill, Ida Caudill, Anna Carter, Margaret Cooper, C. E. Dillon, Frank Havens, Allie Jane Havens, Maud Hogge, John Will Holbrook, Dorothy Holbrook, Leora Hurt, Blanche Jeffrey, N. E. Kennard, Warren Lappin, Ruth Lappin, Arye Lewis, Ottie Nickell, Maud Oppenhiemer, Pruda Garey, Ethel Patton, Clella Porter, E. L. Raybourn, Mrs. E. L. Raybourn, Otto Razor, Clara Robinson, Myrtle Ruley, Cleff Tussey, Ora Waltz, Mayme Wiley, Ruby Woods, Dr. Adron Doran and Mrs. Adron Doran.
Courtesy of Rowan County Public Library

Best friends on graduation from Pikeville High School, 1956. From left to right: James Coleman, Jimmy Dale Anderson and Bill Duty.
Courtesy of Barbara Coleman

1956 graduating class of Pikeville High School. Jimmy Leslie was the class president, Barbara Thompson was vice president, Barbara Sue Childers was secretary and Gail Scott was treasurer. *Courtesy of Barbara Coleman*

Pikeville High School Sallie Dotson class, November 1956. *Courtesy of Pikeville Public Library, Paul B. Mays Collection*

Senior trip from Pikeville High School, 1956. The group is at Marineland, Florida. Kneeling in front are Frankie Biliter and David Elliott. Second row: Bill McCoy, Jackie Layne, Bill Duty, Jody Dorton and Wayne Rutherford. Back row: Everette Justice, Nelson Radwan, James Coleman, Raleigh Wright and Bill Scott. *Courtesy of Barbara Coleman*

Eastern Kentucky schoolroom, circa 1960. *Courtesy of Photographic Archives, Appalachian Learning Laboratory, Alice Lloyd College*

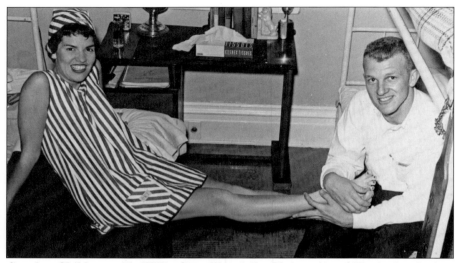

Carolyn Childers with Willie Spradlin at the University of Kentucky during a Phi Kappa Tau weekend slumber party 1957. She was from Pikeville; he was from Prestonsburg. During the slumber party, the girls moved in to the fraternity house, were given nightwear to wear and slept in the boys' beds. The boys spent the night elsewhere. *Courtesy of Carolyn M. Childers*

Sixth-grade class of Advance School, Flatwoods, on a day trip to historic sites in Kentucky including Henry Clay's home, Fort Harrod, the Lincoln Memorial and the State Capitol, 1958. Included are Betty and Bonnie Phelps, Connie Dickerson, Judy Duty, Martha and Sophia Webb, Betty Jo Argabrite, Marcheta Glazier, Kay Conlon, Glenda Greene, Hattie Yates, Helen Metz, Sharon Justice, Charles Nance, Laura Williams, Betty Jo Stevens and teacher Bessie Howes. *Courtesy of Betty Sharp*

Classroom at Wheelwright, 1956. *Courtesy of Photographic Archives, Appalachian Learning Laboratory, Alice Lloyd College*

Scaffold Cane School, 1959. *Courtesy of Appalachian Photoarchives, Southern Appalachian Archives, Berea College*

Alice Lloyd, 1961. Originally from Boston, Alice Lloyd moved to Knott County, Kentucky, in 1916. Overcoming physical handicaps from a bout with polio, Lloyd worked passionately for social reform. During this time a local land owner on Caney Creek offered her part of his land in trade for educating his children. Lloyd used this land to found a model community in Appalachia which started with the Caney Creek Community Center. She named her Caney Creek home "Pippa Passes" after a poem by Robert Browning and in honor of donors from the New England Browning Society. Later Lloyd, her mother, assistant June Buchanan and local volunteers built Caney High School in 1919 with donated money. Together with June Buchanan, Lloyd went on to found 100 elementary schools throughout eastern Kentucky and opened Caney Junior College in 1923. The college offered a free education to mountain youth who were required to promise to remain in the region or return after completing their education. Lloyd served the college until her death in 1962. After her death, the college was renamed in her honor.

Courtesy of Photographic Archives, Appalachian Learning Laboratory, Alice Lloyd College

Pikeville High School's 1961 graduating class. On the left in front is principal Charles Spears with senior class sponsor Gene Davis behind him. On the right is senior class sponsor Maudie Keesee. *Courtesy of Ann E. Carty*

Clement Sowards, 1962, was a teacher at Pikeville High School for 25 years. *Courtesy of Patty Leslie Sowards*

Pikeville High School's senior class trip to Daytona Beach, 1961. Front row, left to right: unidentified, Sally Williamson, unidentified, Mary Hambley, unidentified, Nancy May, unidentified, Toni Goodman, Janis Kidd, Nancy Conway, unidentified, unidentified and Eloise Newsome. Girls kneeling: Pam Venters, Carole Romer, Dawes Miller, Paige Smallwood and Vonna Billiter. Back row: unidentified, Larry Chaney, Gary Yarus, Christine Goodman, Bob Slone, unidentified, Raymond Setser, Walter Hatcher, Ronnie Smith, Danny Lemon, Jack Jones, Bob Venters, Jay Justice, unidentified, Bob Boyce, unidentified, Loren Williams, Donnie Queen, Haskell Mullins, James Cook, unidentified and Scotty Cline. *Courtesy of Ann E. Carty*

Dorm room at Alice Lloyd College, 1962. *Courtesy of Photographic Archives, Appalachian Learning Laboratory, Alice Lloyd College*

McDowell School eighth-grade class, 1962. Holding the sign in the front row, left to right, are David Collins, Randy Smith and Danny King. *Courtesy of Randy Smith*

Becknerville School sixth grade, Winchester, 1964–65. Jonathan D. Adams is in the middle row on the left. *Courtesy of Mary Hamilton Adams*

Fifth-grade class at Becknerville School, Winchester, 1964–65. Timothy G. Adams is in the back row second from the right next to the teacher, Mr. Hahn. *Courtesy of Mary Hamilton Adams*

Pikeville High School Keyette Club, Feb. 9, 1965. Front row, left to right: Frankie Crew, Karin Watson and Carolyn Charles. Second row: Beverly Beeler Sanders, Cherry Lynn May, Jennifer Crickmen, Betsy Jo Venters, Kathy Phillips, Bonni Lynn Bevens, Jane Craig Fields, Billie Jean Allen, Donita Penson and Jean Williamson. Third row: Nancy Combs, Patty Wells, Janie Smith, Madge Walters Baird, Susie Butcher, Alice Baker, Winnie Stone, Jo Cassady, Catherine Lee Benedict, Kay McNeil and Brenda Franklin. *Courtesy of Pikeville Public Library, Paul B. Mays Collection*

Students at Alice Lloyd College, circa 1965. *Courtesy of Photographic Archives, Appalachian Learning Laboratory, Alice Lloyd College*

Typing class at Pikeville High School, circa 1965. *Courtesy of Pikeville Public Library, Paul B. Mays Collection*

Students of Naomi R. Herald's second-grade class of Marie Roberts Elementary School at Lost Creek, Breathitt County, 1965. Front row, left to right: Daisy Francis, Martha Jo Watts, Philip King, Charles Watts, Cleta Fugate, Michele White, Tina McElveen, Grace Herald, Donald Estep, Serena Sizemore and Darlene Strong. Second row: Roger Neace, Naomi R. Herald, Carol Fields, Mary Turner, Judy Wells, Susan Neace, Charles Ray Noble, Claude Strong Jr., Jay D. White, Sidney Gwin, Mary Lou Fields, Patty Deaton and Gail Combs. Third row: Geneva Neace, Bennie Costello, Leonard White, Jeffrey Strong, James Noble, Barbara Noble, Wanda Neace, Eva Mae Spicer, Ronnie Morris, Albert Hollon and Billy Ray Jones. *Courtesy of Carol Fields Shepherd*

An Appalachian schoolroom, circa 1965. *Courtesy of Appalachian Photoarchives, Southern Appalachian Archives, Berea College*

Graduating class of Tyner High School, Jackson County, 1966. *Courtesy of Rosita Morgan Shields*

Whitesburg High School band, 1968. The band director is Alan Siegal. Judy Maggard is in the fourth row on the left. *Courtesy of Judy Burroughs*

Nancy Hurst during her sophomore year at Eastern Kentucky University, Richmond, 1967. The Student Union building is in the background. Nancy later became a local radio personality known as Nancy Plum. *Courtesy of Nancy Plum*

Alice Lloyd College students at the United States Capitol with Sen. John Sherman Cooper, 1966. *Courtesy of Photographic Archives, Appalachian Learning Laboratory, Alice Lloyd College*

Alice Lloyd College students, circa 1968. *Courtesy of Photographic Archives, Appalachian Learning Laboratory, Alice Lloyd College*

Retirement party for Morehead University faculty, June 1969. From left to right: Warren Lappin, Ruth Lappin, W. H. "Honie" Rice, Virginia Rice, Bob Laughlin, Frances Laughlin, Bob Day and Lorene Day. *Courtesy of Lucien H. Rice*

Former Kentucky governor Bert T. Combs stepping from the helicopter that brought him to Alice Lloyd College where he is a visiting lecturer on "The American Political Process," Sept. 20, 1967. Shaking hands with Combs is Miss Jo Hern of the college staff. Other students and faculty are waiting to greet Combs who arrived by helicopter onto the campus that still had mail brought in by mule back. *Courtesy of Photographic Archives, Appalachian Learning Laboratory, Alice Lloyd College*

Homecoming at Alice Lloyd College, 1970. Left to right starting in front: Warren Watson, Rilda Watson, Alice Slone and president of the college Mr. Hayes. Alice was a protégé of Alice Lloyd and started Cordia School. *Courtesy of Pam Stenulson*

RELIGION

Religion has been central to the social fabric of Eastern Kentucky. In some places, it seemed there was at least one church up every hollow, with congregations regularly splitting or regrouping over some personal or doctrinal difference or agreement.

Here you will find Bible study groups and a second-grade class at a Catholic school in Cumberland. Spend some time looking at the faces on those Sundays when an entire congregation posed in front of their church.

The photos in this section range from the baptism of an infant — the son of a coal mine official — in a church, to old-style immersions that took place in a conveniently flat-bottomed creek or river.

There also is an image of worshipers in a Pentecostal church in Harlan County handling a deadly rattlesnake during a service, a practice that continues to this day among those who take literally the Biblical passage that calls on the faithful to "pick up snakes with their hands."

Baptism in Fern Creek in Bell County, circa 1955. *Courtesy of Appalachian Photoarchives, Southern Appalachian Archives, Berea College*

Revival meeting, circa 1940. *Courtesy of Photographic Archives, Appalachian Learning Laboratory, Alice Lloyd College*

Congregation of the Church of God, Vanceburg, 1942. Naomi Hamilton is in the second row fourth from the right. Mary Hamilton is in the third row back near the center with pigtails. *Courtesy of Mary Hamilton Adams*

Sunday school class at Slick Ford School, Estill County, 1941. Sitting in front are Clyde Osborne and Clay Winkle. Standing, left to right: Finley Richardson, Lucille Estes, Ruth Miller, Lillian Estes, Irene Winkle, Donald Richardson, Alpha Winkle, Minnie Estes, Ruth Arvin, Reta Winkle, Armeda Fowler behind Ruth and Reta, Elizabeth Morris, Daisy Mae Brinegar, Ethel Messer, Gladys Sparks and Glenna Osborne. *Courtesy of Wilma Osborne Hamilton*

Christian Church, Morehead, circa 1945. *Courtesy of Camden-Carroll Library, Morehead State University, Roger W. Barbour Collection*

Bible school at First Baptist Church, Barbourville, 1946. First and second rows, left to right: unidentified, unidentified, Jimmy Engle, unidentified, Jim Prichard, unidentified, unidentified, James Arthur Evans, unidentified, unidentified, Hank Mitchell, unidentified, unidentified, Janice Bennett, Marcia Mackey, unidentified, unidentified, Doug Gibson, unidentified, Milton Lay, Euna Fay Hammons, unidentified, Bobby Harp, John R. Wharton, unidentified, unidentified, Paul Kidd, Shirley Joyce Childs, Bobby Ray Jarvis and Rev. Vorse. Third row: Rev. H. C. Childs, unidentified, unidentified, Jerry Lawson, Martha Clouse, Mildred Hammons, Brenda Gilpin, Pat Disney, Eva Woolum, unidentified, Larry Hammons, Carl Tedders, Mary Alice Lay, Barbara K. Evans, Wanda Warfield, Nick Melton, Anita McNeil, unidentified and Betty Ann Collier. Fourth row: unidentified, unidentified, unidentified, unidentified, Emily Picard, Shirley Ann Stewart, Joan Clouse, Sam Melton, Sandra Hammons, Deana Prichard, Jackie Partin, Mary Clenens Tye, unidentified, Francis Fox, Norma Jo Collier and Inez Buttery. Fifth row: Jimmy Bays, Jim Bill Jones, unidentified, unidentified, Leroy McNeil, unidentified, Jerry Holifield, unidentified, Doris Jean Davis, Billy Ray Lawson, Hobart Creasy, Willard Morris and John Elswick. Sixth row: Patsy Tydings, Mariam Disney, unidentified, Carla Jean Sutton, unidentified, Norma McDonald, Beulah Fortney, Margaret Jane Simpson, Lou Ann Bays, Doris Jean Carter, Patsy Warfield, (unknown) Payne and Harvey Maybrier. Seventh row: Teddy Steel, unidentified, Paul Osborne, Glen Sargent, Marion Hurd, Charlie Bill Ensslin, (unknown) Bonner, Billy Taylor, Lawrence Stewart, Gary Martin, unidentified, W. C. Sargent, unidentified, Ray Evans, Francine Orick, Rosemary Fortney, Don Corey, unidentified, Russ Higgins, unidentified, unidentified and unidentified. Eighth and ninth rows: Betty Buttery, Peggy Lumpkins, Cora Bell Williams, Joyce Prichard, Jerry Elswick, Louise Walker, Mareka Disney, Barbara Tye, Sybil Parsons, Patsy Bays, Patricia Voorhees, Betty Jean Walker, Noma Osborne, Peggy Warfield, Louise Hurd, Jimmie Sue Bateman, (unknown) Lovett and Nancy Melton. Tenth row: Mrs. T. J. Jarvis, Angie Miracle, Alice Parrott, Jennie Chestnut, Beatrice Hughes, teacher Mrs. Morris, Virginia Pierce, Martha Poff, Jerry Easterly Walker, Mrs. Payne, Mary Catherine Morris, unidentified and Beatice Hubbard. *Courtesy of Pat and Don Dampier*

Handling serpents at the Pentecostal Church of God, PV & K Coal Co., Clover Gap Mine, Lejunior, Harlan County, Sept. 15, 1946. Most of the members were coal miners and their families. *Courtesy of Photographic Archives, Appalachian Learning Laboratory, Alice Lloyd College*

Church of God Bible school, Morehead, 1947. *Courtesy of Camden-Carroll Library, Morehead State University, Roger W. Barbour Collection*

Outside Liberty Ave. Baptist Church after the church was built by Rev. James R. Prince in the late 1940s. *Courtesy of Jim Prince*

Choir at the Methodist Church, Wheelwright, Sept. 22, 1946. Rev. Jackson is at his pulpit. *Courtesy of Photographic Archives, Appalachian Learning Laboratory, Alice Lloyd College*

Henry Morgan being baptized in Jackson County, 1949. *Courtesy of Rosita Morgan Shields*

Saint Stephen Catholic School second-grade class, Cumberland, 1952. Front row, fourth from the left: Karen Cook. Second row, fourth from the left: Jimmy Sepe. Third row, third from the left: Sophia Kozlovik Owada. *Courtesy of Sam Owada*

Louisa Methodist Church, circa 1952. The funeral of Fred Vinson was held in this church in 1953. *Courtesy of Linda Fugitt*

Blue Lick Baptist Church, circa 1954. The church was started by Rev. James Reuben Prince. *Courtesy of Jim Prince*

Binghamtown Baptist Church, circa 1955. *Courtesy of Bell County Historical Society*

Blue Lick Baptist Church, circa 1954. Patricia Marie Prince is on the left end of the second pew in the checkered dress. Her father, Rev. James R. Prince, was the pastor and organizer of the church. *Courtesy of Jim Prince*

Ferristown Church, Berea, circa 1955. *Courtesy of Appalachian Photoarchives, Southern Appalachian Archives, Berea College*

Sunday school class from Flemingsburg Christian Church, 1955. The teacher on the far left is Opal Arnold; the teacher on the right is Hazel Williams. In the front row, the girl sitting third from the right is Ann Tevis. In the front row, the first girl on the left is Paula Cheap with Calvin Cheap behind her and to the right. Gary Waddell is the sixth boy from the right in the back row.

Courtesy of Opal Waddell

Baptism of Charles Stuart Steele Jr. at the Lynch Church of the Resurrection, April 1957. From left to right: Rev. Wagner, Charles Stuart Steele Sr., T. E. Johnson and Mrs. T. E. Johnson holding Charles. T. E. Johnson was the superintendent of U.S. Steel Mines at Lynch at that time. *Courtesy of Billie M. Steele*

Confirmation class, Saint Stephen Catholic Church, Cumberland, 1957. Front row, third and fourth from the left: Louise Perkins and Kathy Kozlovik Owada. Second row, first on the left: Diane Saltess. Third row, fourth from the left: Tommy Kelemen. *Courtesy of Sam Owada*

First Presbyterian Church, Middlesboro, circa 1958. *Courtesy of Bell County Historical Society*

Buckhorn Presbyterian Church, Perry County, 1961. *Courtesy of Bobby Davis Museum and Park*

Sunday school group at Saylor Branch, Church of God, Dec. 27, 1959. Rev. John Hamilton, pastor, is in the fourth row back on the left. His wife, Mae, is in front of him. *Courtesy of Mary Hamilton Adams*

Sunday school class at Frenchburg Baptist Church, Easter Sunday, 1962. From left to right: teacher Bertha Mae Day, Dorothy Buchanan, Charlotte Craig, Gwendolyn Stull, Patty Lisle, Janelle Frye and Dinah Smith. *Courtesy of Dorothy Hunter*

Ladies Aid Society of the Advance Memorial Church, Flatwoods, circa 1960. From left to right: Mary Turner, Joyce Turner, Delcie Nance, Capitola "Cappy" Phelps and Gladys Clark. *Courtesy of Betty Sharp*

First Baptist Church of Hazard on their annual church picnic at Bobby Davis Memorial Park, circa 1965. On the left in the white shirt is Moscoe Blackburn; behind him is his wife, Wynona. *Courtesy of Vickie Blackburn*

Saint Stephen Catholic School eighth-grade graduation, Cumberland, 1961. Second row, left to right: Richard Kirk, Kathy Kozlovik Owada, Joe Creech, Diane Saltess and Tommy Kelemen. The front row is unidentified. *Courtesy of Sam Owada*

First Presbyterian Church, Hazard, Cultural Enrichment Program participants, 1968. Vickie Blackburn is standing next to the sign on the left; Missy Mitchell is among the children on the left; Lynn Greer is to the right of the sign. The three young woman are the teachers. *Courtesy of Vickie Blackburn*

Union Church Bible school, Berea, circa 1965. *Courtesy of Appalachian Photoarchives, Southern Appalachian Archives, Berea College*

FAMILY & FRIENDS

Eastern Kentucky has always been about family.

Because of a terrain that both pushed people together along creeks and rivers and isolated them from people in the next watershed over the ridge, neighbors and kin developed a closeness not often found in some other parts of the country.

And, as you will see on the following pages, there was something about people coming together that seemed to bring out a camera. A wedding, a funeral, a new bicycle, a slumber party, working in the fields, a big snow, Christmas at Mamaw and Papaw's house — it all was preserved for posterity. Family reunions also drew photographers, and so did just getting a single family together. That was no small feat in the days when mother, father and the children created a crowd of a dozen or more people.

The Fortner family, Berea, circa 1940. *Courtesy of Kathryn Freeman*

Georgia and Shirl Huffman with baby Dean Huffman in the shade of their porch, Rockhouse in Pike County, 1940. *Courtesy of Marsha Koller*

From left to right, sisters Nell Ruth Morris, Louise Childers and Josephine Childers, all received fur coats for Christmas, circa 1940. They all lived in Pikeville. *Courtesy of Carolyn M. Childers*

Young family, Estill County, circa 1942, shortly after the funeral of Willie Sr.'s wife. Girls in front, left to right: unidentified, unidentified and Lillie Tilghman. Adults in the back row: Tilldarene, husband Willie Jr., Willie Sr., Mrs. Walker Young, Walker Young and Alice Young Tilghman. Willie Jr. and Walker are the children of Willie Sr. Alice is the daughter of Tilldarene and Willie Jr. Lillie is daughter of Alice. After her death, Willie Sr.'s wife was laid out in the family home for the review and wake. The next morning, the casket had to be carried over this bridge to the church for the funeral and burial. *Courtesy of Lillie Tilghman Cox*

Sarah Margaret Poplin Fox at her 86th birthday party at Denniston, 1940. *Courtesy of Dorothy Hunter*

William Coldiron and Virginia Woodward's wedding day at Crummies, 1940. *Courtesy of Sarah Coldiron Camden*

Florence "Hebads" Hall Sizemore holds her grandson, Barry Martin, with her granddaughter, Pluma Martin, at her side at Weeksbury Coal Camp, 1941. *Courtesy of Barry and Magnolia Martin*

Powers family, Morehead, circa 1940. Emma Jane Garrison Powers and John Harlan Powers are seated in front. Back row, left to right: Katherine, Lottie, Tom, Ernestine and Norma. *Courtesy of Rowan County Public Library*

Neighborhood toddlers, Pikeville, 1940. In the rocking chair is Jimmy Leslie, in the stroller in front is Barbara Sue Childers and in the high chair is Bill Scott. *Courtesy of Patty Leslie Sowards*

Miners' wives and children on the front porch at Kentucky Straight Creek Coal Co., Belva Mine, Bell County, Four Mile, Sept. 4, 1946. *Courtesy of Photographic Archives, Appalachian Learning Laboratory, Alice Lloyd College*

Berea College women at the Ogg residence on Jackson Street in Berea, circa 1940. The younger girl is Wilma Lou Fortner, granddaughter of Coleman and Nora Ogg. The Oggs had a photography studio in town. The Ogg family, starting with Coleman "Coley" Ogg in 1888, photographed life in Berea and throughout Eastern Kentucky for about 75 years. *Courtesy of Kathryn Freeman*

Tivis and Dessie Patrick family gathering at the Tivis Patrick home in Olive Hill, Carter County, circa 1944. From left to right: unidentified, Ruby Planck, Norman Patrick, Tivis Patrick, Dessie Patrick with Gary in front of her, Burgess Patrick, Mae Hamilton with Thomas in front of her and Angeline Planck. *Courtesy of Mary Hamilton Adams*

Four generations of Hall men, 1941. In the center is James Emery Hall. On the right is his son, Milford. Milford's son, Edgille, is on the left. The two boys in front are Ronnie, left, and Eddie Leslie, Milford's grandsons. *Courtesy of Opal Waddell*

Five generations of the Ray family, circa 1941. In front, left to right: Tabitha Myers Ray, widow of Confederate Civil War soldier James Wesley Ray; Ray Phelps; and Rose Ray Phelps. In back are Minnie Ray Phelps and Charles Ralph Phelps. *Courtesy of Bonnie Phelps Sweatman*

Billie Lynn, Barbara Sue and Carolyn Childers sledding in Carolyn's yard in Pikeville, 1942. *Courtesy of Carolyn M. Childers*

Nell Ruth Morris with her three nieces: Billie Lynn, Barbara Sue and Carolyn Childers, 1941. On the left in back is Carolyn's playhouse at their home in Pikeville. *Courtesy of Carolyn M. Childers*

Clyde Osborne with daughter Wilma and brother Robert Lee "Bobby" Osborne, Estill County, 1944. *Courtesy of Wilma Osborne Hamilton*

The Young family in front of their home in Flatwoods, 1945. In front are Cappy Young Phelps with son Ray, left, and Clara Young McNeil holding daughter Cookie. In back are Illa and Herman Young, parents of Cappy and Clara. *Courtesy of Betty Sharp*

Hamp and Mary Wooten at their home in Cumberland, circa 1943. Hamp was a miner for U.S. Steel. Their children are Beuna, in front, and Arzona. *Courtesy of Beuna Wooten*

Mrs. Roy Terry with her two daughters and Bess Turner in Jackson, 1948. *Courtesy of Kathy Carter*

Dr. and Mrs. O. M. Lyons and family at home, circa 1945. *Courtesy of Camden-Carroll Library, Morehead State University, Roger W. Barbour Collection*

Osborne family at the Jake and Bessie Osborne home down on the river at Palmer, Estill County, 1944. Wilma is in the wash basin with her uncle, Bobby, watching her. On the steps is father Clyde and grandma Bessie. *Courtesy of Wilma Osborne Hamilton*

Coldiron family at Crummies in Harlan County, 1948, left to right: Virginia, Sarah and Maxine. *Courtesy of Sarah Coldiron Camden*

M. J. Hall with Eddie Leslie, Opal Hall with Ronnie Leslie, Birdie Hall and Alta Leslie in Flemingsburg, 1945. *Courtesy of Opal Waddell*

Earl Bradley's birthday party, Rowan County, circa 1945. *Courtesy of Camden-Carroll Library, Morehead State University, Roger W. Barbour Collection*

Clyde and Armeda Osborne with their daughter, Wilma Lee, at their home near The Forks, Estill County, 1944. Clyde's father, Jake Osborne, is on the front porch. Their dog's name was Jack. *Courtesy of Wilma Osborne Hamilton*

Mrs. Monroe Jones cooks while her daughter watches in their home at Bell County, Four Mile, Sept. 4, 1946. The family paid $9.75 a month for rent. *Courtesy of Photographic Archives, Appalachian Learning Laboratory, Alice Lloyd College*

Andrew Broughton with some of the 315 quarts of fruit and vegetables that his wife had canned throughout the summer, Aug. 31, 1946. They lived at Fox Ridge Mining Co., Inc., Hanby Mine, Arjay, Bell County. *Courtesy of Photographic Archives, Appalachian Learning Laboratory, Alice Lloyd College*

Mrs. Sergent pours the bath water for her husband, Sept. 13, 1946. The company, PV & K Coal Co., Clover Gap Mine, Lejunior, Harlan County, had no bathhouse and no running water in any of the houses. *Courtesy of Photographic Archives, Appalachian Learning Laboratory, Alice Lloyd College*

Wedding of Opal Hall and Lloyd Waddell at the Flemingsburg Baptist Church, 1947. From left to right: Glenna Waddell, Alta Leslie, Opal, Lloyd, Don Clare, John David and Glenn Lenzer. The minister is Rev. Jones. *Courtesy of Opal Waddell*

Pat Disney on her first bicycle, 1948. She and her cousin, Jimmy Engle, are in their grandmother's backyard in Barbourville. *Courtesy of Pat and Don Dampier*

Benjamin and Katherine Hurst by their home on Walnut Street, Richmond. Mr. Hurst was one of the first plumbers in Eastern Kentucky, founding the Richmond Motor and Plumbing Co. with A.C. Scanlan in 1908. Mr. Hurst died shortly after this picture was taken in 1949. *Courtesy of Nancy Plum*

The Henry and Opal Morgan family, Jackson County, 1949. In front, left to right: Cleda, Delphine and Evelyn. In back are Henry, holding Rosita, and Opal. *Courtesy of Rosita Morgan Shields*

Neighborhood children visiting their teacher, Pauline Allen, at her home on a Sunday, McDowell, circa 1948. Front row, left to right: unidentified, Richard Sammons and Dennise Hall. Middle row: Vera Parsons, Barry Martin and unidentified. Back row: Shannon Parson, Tony Elam and the teacher's son, Ray Allen. *Courtesy of Barry Dean Martin*

Betsy Francis, "Queen for a Day," and Hugh Dunbar from WKIC Radio at the entrance to Bobby Davis Park, 1949. Betsy came from California to Hazard to visit her parents. She drove this 1949 Frazier while she was in town. *Courtesy of Bobby Davis Museum and Park*

Mida H. King farming in Salsbury, circa 1949. *Courtesy of Wally King Hinton*

The Buchanan sisters at Rothwell, 1949. They were called to stop their play for a quick photograph taken by a family friend. From youngest to oldest: Dorothy, Mary, Phyllis, Doris and Faye. Mary has a handful of Easter lillies she had just picked. *Courtesy of Dorothy Hunter*

Shaler "Pops" and Laura Gilliam, Cumberland, circa 1958. The Gilliam family was one of the pioneering families of the Cumberland area. *Courtesy of Sam Owada*

Pikeville friends, 1949, left to right: Geraldine Bevins, Barbara Damron, Gail Hilton, Lois Coleman and Patty Leslie. *Courtesy of Patty Leslie Sowards*

Cappy Phelps with her son, Ray, in front of their home in Flatwoods, circa 1950. *Courtesy of Betty Sharp*

Chester Hamilton and his son, Chester Lewis Hamilton, Hargett. The truck is a 1949 Chevrolet. *Courtesy of Wilma Osborne Hamilton*

Hay stacks on the Rev. Henry Clay and Sally Fields farm, Lost Creek, Breathitt County, circa 1950. Between them is their niece, Thelma Grigsby Watts. *Courtesy of Carol Fields Shepherd*

George and Marie Smith of Flatwoods with their sons, 1952. George is holding Greg with Randy in front of his mother. *Courtesy of Randy Smith*

King family farming in Salsbury, circa 1949, left to right: Frank, Tee and Edward with their father, Walter. *Courtesy of Wally King Hinton*

The four daughters of Henry and Opal Morgan, Jackson County, 1951. In front, left to right: Rosita and Cleda. In back: Delphine and Evelyn. Opal helped her husband with the farmwork and milked their cow, mowed the lawn, made two hot meals a day, washed their clothes with a wringer washer and grew and canned the produce from a large garden. She also sewed all the clothes for her four daughters, her mother and herself. She also crocheted, was active in Homemakers, sold Avon and sang and played guitar for their church. *Courtesy of Rosita Morgan Shields*

Rosita, Cleda, Evelyn, in the background, and Delphine Morgan fishing on their farm, Jackson County, 1951. *Courtesy of Rosita Morgan Shields*

John and Sarah Lewis and children, Rowan County, 1951. *Courtesy of Camden-Carroll Library, Morehead State University, Roger W. Barbour Collection*

Henry Morgan on his Farmall Cub, Jackson County, 1952. *Courtesy of Rosita Morgan Shields*

Wilma Lee Osbourne with her neighbor, Billy Elliott, and his pony, Dolly, in Stump, Estill County, 1952. The school Wilma attended is in the background. *Courtesy of Wilma Osborne Hamilton*

Sam Owada celebrating his fourth birthday at their home in Cumberland, 1953. From left to right: Nicky March, Ronnie Begley, sister Sophia, Sam, sister Kathy and cousin Jimmy Sepe. *Courtesy of Sam Owada*

Sandy, Judy, Pam, Anna Lou, Linda and Bobby Maggard eating fresh apples on Big Cowan, Whitesburg, July 1954. Sisters Sandy and Pam are cousins visiting from Michigan. *Courtesy of Judy Burroughs*

Barbara Lou Grace Sing Bowling with her daughters, Frances, age nine, and JoAnn, age 17, Middlesboro, May 1953. Barbara died of cancer five years later. *Courtesy of Frances J. Taylor*

Odell Moses and Betty Seale in the backyard of Betty's parents' home in Cawood, circa 1953. Odell and Betty were courting and later married. *Courtesy of T. J. Seale*

Classmates from Barbourville High School, 1954. From left to right: Norma Jo Collier, Ruth Mills, Jackie Hyde and Pat Disney. They are on College Street in front of the Union College president's home. *Courtesy of Pat and Don Dampier*

Marsh Bellomy in Breaks Interstate Park between Pike County, Kentucky, and Virginia, 1956. His fiancé, Patti Huffman, snapped this picture right after he asked her to marry him. *Courtesy of Marsha Koller*

Home of Howard and Sally Williams on Cram Creek, Letcher County, circa 1957. It sits on the North Fork of the Kentucky River. *Courtesy of Michael Wells*

Faye Shepherd and son Willard Ray in front of their clothesline full of diapers, 1954. They lived at Lunah in Breathitt County. *Courtesy of Carol Fields Shepherd*

Clyde Osborne, left, and J. B. Fowler swinging Melanie Fowler at the Elbert Fowler home in Estill County, August 1957. In the back are Terry Fowler and Gary Gilmore. *Courtesy of Wilma Osborne Hamilton*

The Smith family of Flatwoods, circa 1958. From left to right: mother Eva Smith, Lucille, George, Ruth Ann, June Lee and Linda. *Courtesy of Randy Smith*

Dewey Martin and grandson Greg Stumbo relax in the backyard in McDowell, circa 1954. *Courtesy of Barry Dean Martin*

Oliver "Perry" Wells with all his children at a Botts and Wells reunion, Denniston, Menifee County, 1958. The children include: Roy, Dewey, Kenneth, Martha, Thelma, Pearlie and Edith. *Courtesy of Dorothy Hunter*

King and Hall family gathering, January 1958. Included are: Edward King, Lucy Hall, Frank King, Bearnice King, Ray King, Elizabeth King, Walter King, Mida King, Gallie Hall, Walter King, Emma King, W. J. King, Silas King, Tee King, Mary King, Shirley King, Betty Hall and Altie Hall. *Courtesy of Wally King Hinton*

Twins Bertha Turner, McDowell, and Birdie Hall, Weeksbury, celebrating their birthday together, circa 1960. *Courtesy of Opal Waddell*

Silas Gayheart, Perry County, 1955. He was very politically active in the Democratic party. When he was hospitalized during the gubernatorial race of Happy Chandler, he got up from his hospital bed, put on his clothes and hat and was taken by ambulance to the voting site at Dwarf Elementary School. After casting his ballot, he returned to his hospital bed. *Courtesy of Phyllis Ann Ritchie Taylor*

Milford and Birdie Hall family gathering in Floyd County, 1960. Seated in front are Birdie and Milford "M. J." with Randy Waddell on his lap. Standing from left to right: Keith Leslie, Gary Waddell, Opal Waddell, Alta Leslie, Larry Leslie and Dr. Ed Leslie. *Courtesy of Opal Waddell*

In Flatwoods, Greenup County, from left to right: Illa Elizabeth Hall Young, Clara Young McNeil, Betty Watson Fogle, Capitola "Cappy" Young Phelps and Ruby Watson Meade, circa 1955. The three women in front grew up together as sisters; the two in back are Illa's daughters. *Courtesy of Betty Sharp*

The Wootens, Gospel singers, circa 1960. They sang in churches throughout Harlan County and surrounding counties including all-day meetings and dinners on the ground. The siblings, left to right: Naomia, Hamp and Arzona. Beuna is in the back. *Courtesy of Beuna Wooten*

Dale Seale sitting on the swing in his front yard in Cawood, circa 1962. He owned the Gulf service station in Cawood. *Courtesy of T. J. Seale*

The children of Raleigh and Faye Shepherd, Blanton Bridge, Breathitt County, enjoy a family outing at Sky Bridge in Wolfe County, July 1961. From left to right: Pamela, Rita, Sheila and Willard Ray. *Courtesy of Carol Fields Shepherd*

Waverly Buchanan and his wife, Delta, and granddaughter Juliana Buchanan with a finished tobacco bed behind them, Rothwell, 1961. *Courtesy of Dorothy Hunter*

Frances Bowling and Walt Taylor at the Jaycee's Fair in Middlesboro, 1961. Frances was a junior in high school; Walt was a senior. They bought their matching shirts at the local Montgomery Ward store. *Courtesy of Frances J. Taylor*

Menefee and Julie Daroset Buchanan working together in their home in Rothwell, 1963. *Courtesy of Dorothy Hunter*

The Colegrove children of Harlan County, 1965. They are in front of their family home at 601 Short Street. Clockwise starting in front: Becky, Tina, Cindy and Cathy. *Courtesy of Ruby Colegrove family*

Ready for the Menifee County High School Talent Show, 1965, from left to right: Mary Buchanan, Dorothy Buchanan and Patty Lisle. *Courtesy of Dorothy Hunter*

Slumber party at the home of Judy Haynes in Hazard, October 1965. On the bottom, left to right: Ella Nora Miller, Gini Watkins and Jean Beeler. On top are Connie Davis and Missy Mitchell. *Courtesy of Vickie Blackburn*

Cousins putting up corn at the Maggard home on Big Cowan, Whitesburg, 1968. *Courtesy of Judy Burroughs*

Raleigh family reunion, Big Cowan, Whitesburg, 1968. *Courtesy of Judy Burroughs*

Willard Maggard and daughter Judy ready for a football game, August 1968, after Willard had put in a day's work in the coal mines. *Courtesy of Judy Burroughs*

Lewis and Wilma Hamilton with their daughters, Sherry and Debbie, at Wilma's grandparents' home at Doe Creek, Estill County, circa 1968. *Courtesy of Wilma Osborne Hamilton*

Dr. Thomas Edward Hamilton, 1966. He graduated from Lewis County High School and the University of Kentucky College of Medicine.

Courtesy of Mary Hamilton Adams

The Blackburn family of Hazard, Christmas 1968. The couple in front is Moscoe and Wynona Blackburn, standing is Wynona's mother, Carlee Little, with the Blackburn's daughter, Regina. *Courtesy of Vickie Blackburn*

Christmas at Mamaw and Papaw Hamilton's house at Hargett, Irvine, 1967. From left to right are cousins: Sherry Hamilton, Deborah Hamilton, Ginger Garrett, Julie Garrett, Robbie Flynn holding Ricky Garrett and Jerry Flynn. *Courtesy of Wilma Osborne Hamilton*

Sherry and Debbie Hamilton with Earl Ray and Jerry Kelly, Wagersville, Irvine, circa 1969. The children played together when Sherry and Debbie visited their grandparents' home at Station Camp in Irvine. *Courtesy of Wilma Osborne Hamilton*

Walter and Frances June Taylor with their son, Walter Marcel "Marc," Middlesboro, December 1970. *Courtesy of Frances J. Taylor*

Wedding rehearsal dinner for Betty Phelps and Bill Sharp held at the Eagles Nest, Morehead, Aug. 8, 1970. From left to right: father of the groom Kenneth Sharp, mother of the bride Cappy Phelps, maid of honor Bonnie Phelps Sweatman, groom Bill Sharp, bride Betty Phelps and best man Ken Sharp. *Courtesy of Betty Sharp*

COMMUNITY

It didn't require a special occasion for people to come together, but occasions were invented anyway.

Festivals were held to show off the corn grown in one county, the honey made in another, or, most famously, the beauty of mountain laurels in full bloom. The '40s, '50s and '60s may have been the heyday for parades. A holiday seldom passed without a march down Main Street that featured lavish floats and what seemed to be every convertible in town.

Eastern Kentuckians came together to form men's civic groups, garden clubs, and Boy Scout troops. In this section you will find the large number of men in suits at a Berea Kiwanis Club meeting and a similar gathering of the Louisa Rotary Club, and a much smaller and more casual group that was the Rowan County Farmer's Club.

Take special note of the headquarters of the Middlesboro Chamber of Commerce: A building constructed of coal.

Berea Kiwanis Club, circa 1940. *Courtesy of Appalachian Photoarchives, Southern Appalachian Archives, Berea College*

"Right Hand Star," Berea Folk Festival, 1941. *Courtesy of Appalachian Photoarchives, Southern Appalachian Archives, Berea College*

Cub Scouts and Boy Scouts of Rowan County, circa 1943. Front row, left to right: unidentified, unidentified, Don Young, Paul George, Billy Joe Wells, Lucien Rice, unidentified, Jim Wellman, William Earl Clay, unidentified and unidentified. Second row: Harold Lancaster, Jerry Riddle, Sonny Jaminson, Andy Aoke, Buddy Kinney, Phillip Ray Cazee, unidentified, J. T. Green, Talmadge Kline, Bob Barber and Jack Barber. Back row: unidentified, Gerald Lancaster, Carl Fair, unidentified, Bill Vaughn, Bill Rice, unidentified and unidentified. *Courtesy of Lucien H. Rice*

Cub Scouts and guests at bingo, Morehead, circa 1945. *Courtesy of Camden-Carroll Library, Morehead State University, Roger W. Barbour Collection*

Rowan County Farmers Club, circa 1945. *Courtesy of Camden-Carroll Library, Morehead State University, Roger W. Barbour Collection*

Parade float for Benham Safety Day, 1947. On the float are Billie Smiddie, left, and Pearl Walters. *Courtesy of anonymous*

Three of Pikeville's belles, Ann Danburg, Gail Hylton and Donna Wheeler, escort a replica of the Liberty Bell in a parade, circa 1950. *Courtesy of Ann E. Carty*

First year the Mountain Laurel Festival was reinstituted following World War II, Pineville, 1949. Billie Smiddie is on the float. The committee putting on the festival sent the girls patterns and material and they had their own dresses made. *Courtesy of anonymous*

Louisa Rotary Club, 1949. Front row, left to right: Kenneth Hayes, W. E. Queen, Alvas See, C. T. Stewart, Newman Marcum, Col. John Poole and Chesley Wright. Second row: Ned Reneau, Bill Keeton, Homer Wright Jr., Lester McHargue, Dr. H. B. Lewis and Lucien Ball. Third row: M. J. See, Dewey Pack, Dan D. Ball, Leon Compton, J. B. Moore and Bill Cheek. Back row: H. H. Curtright, L. L. Lycan, Arch McClure, J. Hager Moore, James Hughes, E. C. Vanhoose and Dr. J. E. Carter Sr. *Courtesy of Linda Fugitt*

Children in the Bobby Davis Library, Hazard, circa 1950. The librarian was Madeline Hay. *Courtesy of Bobby Davis Museum and Park*

The coal house in Middlesboro served as an office for the Chamber of Commerce, circa 1950. The building was constructed totally of coal. *Courtesy of Bell County Historical Society*

Daniel Boone Festival parade around Court Square in Barbourville, circa 1950. *Courtesy of Pat and Don Dampier*

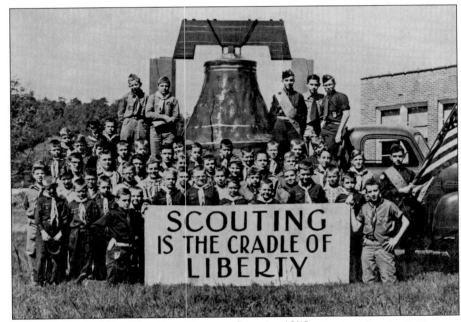

Cub Scouts and Boy Scouts of Rowan County, 1950. *Courtesy of Lucien H. Rice*

Rowan County Eagle Court of Honor, September 1951. Front row, left to right: Don Blair, Dale Hutchinson, unidentified, Bill Pierce and Bob Meader. Back row: Harold Bedenbaugh, Don Young, Lucien Rice and Dale Fair. *Courtesy of Lucien H. Rice*

Construction of the Memorial Gymnasium, Hazard, 1951. When the community of Hazard began planning to build a field house that would have required debt of a million dollars, Lawrence O. Davis stepped in. He located a site almost under the doorstep of the high school's back door that had been overlooked by others, then he went to work to secure the land and make plans. He solicited donations from community members and took on the job of overseeing the work himself to save the cost of a contractor. The gymnasium was opened and dedicated in September 1951 with a seating capacity of over 4,000 and a debt of less than $75,000. *Courtesy of Bobby Davis Museum and Park*

Tea in the home of Elizabeth and Henry Curtright, Louisa, following the dedication of the Vancouver Marker at the Louisa-Fort Gay bridge, circa 1950. The events were sponsored by the Louisa Chapter, Daughters of the American Revolution, while Elizabeth was serving as regent. The marker honored the first white child born in the Eastern Kentucky area. Elizabeth is second from the right with her husband, Henry H. Curtright, fifth from the right. Chief Justice Fred Vinson was also present to dedicate the marker. He is third from the right with his wife, Roberta, fourth from the right. *Courtesy of Linda Fugitt*

May Festival in Barbourville, 1954. The royalty is seated on the steps at Union College. Starting in front and going up the steps: Margie Seale, Malloney Asher, Louise Jones, Patsy Williamson, Nellie Barnes, Jackie Partin, Pat Disney, Jackie Hyde, Georgia McDonald, Norma Collier, Ruth Mills, maid of honor Eleanor Carruth, May queen Beverly McDonald and Coy Prichard. Officer Jim Smith is in back on the left. In front of the steps on the left are Jerry Walker and retiring queen Aline Swaford. Pudd Foley is at the microphone. *Courtesy of Pat and Don Dampier*

Peach Orchard Players, Pikeville, present "The Night of January 21st," 1951. Front row, left to right: Mayme Amick, Paul Mayes, Patty Preston Auxier and Otta Danburg Barton. Second row: Jim Bogardus, Mary Frances Blalock, Irene Spence, Lois Ann Bevins, Mary Evelyn Rogers, Fayne Hughes, Mary Ellen Evans, Lucille Sowards and Dr. Hugh Smith. Third row: Levi Coleman, Ed Venters, John M. Stambaugh, Dr. Charles Rutledge, Thurman Hibbitts, Dr. Bob Bevins, Frank Ramsey, Ernie Rogers and Pearl Hyden. *Courtesy of Ann E. Carty*

Mt. Laurel Festival in Pineville, 1954. The queen candidate riding in the car is Jimmie Sue Bateman. She was from Barbourville and was representing Eastern Kentucky State College. *Courtesy of Pat and Don Dampier*

May Festival in Barbourville, 1954. On the float from left to right: Patsy Williamson, Jackie Hyde, Ruth Mills, Pat Disney, Nellie Barnes, Norma Collier and 1953 Queen Aline Swafford. *Courtesy of Pat and Don Dampier*

Contestants for the Perry County Homecoming Queen, Hazard, 1954. *Courtesy of Photographic Archives, Appalachian Learning Laboratory, Alice Lloyd College*

The Hazard High School marching band on East Main Street and High Street, 1954. The Standard Oil service station is on the left. Some of the businesses on the right side of the street are the CocaCola Bottling Co., Crown Hotel, Shafter Combs and Son Plumbing and Heating and The Wheel. *Courtesy of Bobby Davis Museum and Park*

Perry County Homecoming Parade in Hazard, 1954. *Courtesy of Photographic Archives, Appalachian Learning Laboratory, Alice Lloyd College*

El Kasa Shriners from Ashland in Pikeville for the Spring Ceremonial, May 15, 1954. *Courtesy of Pikeville Public Library, Paul B. Mays Collection*

Troop 25 of McDowell attend Shawnee Scout Camp at Dewey Lake, circa 1955. Left to right: Ballard Jones Jr., Clive Akers Jr., Kenneth Castle, Barry Dean Martin, Kenneth Akers, scoutmaster Woodrow Castle, Sam Martin II and Ed Patton. *Courtesy of Frank Salyers*

Women dressed for the centennial celebration in 1956, Morehead. Seated is Sydney Lane. Standing, left to right: Mrs. J. Roger Caudill, Beulah Williams, Edith Crosley and Marguerite Jayne. *Courtesy of Rowan County Public Library*

Morehead Centennial Parade, 1956. *Courtesy of Rowan County Public Library*

Business and Professional Women, BPW, representatives with the mayor of Hazard, circa 1960. From left to right: Bonnie Seale, Mary Morgan and Mayor Doug Combs. *Courtesy of Bobby Davis Museum and Park*

Beta Sigma Phi Sorority, Cumberland, 1958, left to right: Louise Lewis, unidentified, Kathleen Stacey, Billie Steele, Marcia Wells, Geneva Creech, Jeannie Reams and Edna Lind. *Courtesy of anonymous*

Mountain View Garden Club, Hazard, 1964. *Courtesy of Bobby Davis Museum and Park*

Hazard Civic Night, 1969. With their awards from left to right: Willard Ashworth, Educator of the Year; Mayor Bill Morton, Man of the Year; and Danny Martin, Young Man of the Year. *Courtesy of Bobby Davis Museum and Park*